CHRISTMAS

WITH

Victoria

2000

CHRISTMAS

WITH

Victoria

2000

Text by Kim Waller

Oxmoor
House.

HEARST COMMUNICATIONS, INC.

Christmas with Victoria *2000*

Oxmoor House, Inc.
Book Division of Southern Progress Corporation
P.O. Box 2463, Birmingham, AL 35201

ISBN: 0-8487-1962-x
ISSN: 1093-7633

Printed in Singapore
First printing 2000

We're here for you!
We at Oxmoor House are dedicated to serving you with reliable information that expands your
imagination and enriches your life. We welcome your comments and suggestions. Please write us at:
Oxmoor House, Inc.
Christmas with Victoria
2100 Lakeshore Drive
Birmingham, AL 35209
To order additional publications, call (205) 877-6560 or visit us at www.oxmoorhouse.com.

For *Victoria* Magazine
Editor in Chief: Nancy Lindemeyer
Art Director: Susan Maher

Editor: Bruce Shostak
Designer: Lynne Yeamans

Produced by Smallwood & Stewart, Inc., New York

c o n t e n t s

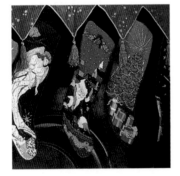

FOREWORD

Amid all the hustle of the holidays, there is a moment when Christmas happens. It may be a carol that suddenly lifts the heart or the jingle of bells on a city street. But for me, Christmas happens when, lifting the wreath to the door, I inhale fresh balsam. Always, that spicy scent brings a rush of memories of all the homes I've lived in and loved.

Home is never dearer to us than during this season of joy and reunion. Though certain rituals, such as the same angel being set atop the tree, may be unbudgeable, many touches are open to pure invention. At *Victoria*, we think about Christmas all year long, devising beautiful ways to bring your home alive with holiday magic. A gardener's wizardry with nature's gifts, a menu that transforms homey favorites into succulent surprises, a tree hung with homemade ribbon stars—there's no end to the ideas you'll find here for creating a holiday as gratifying to you as to the family and friends who share it. Whether you polish antique silver or snip ornaments from tinfoil, you'll find ways to brighten your home. Many of the materials you need to create these stunning decorations are readily available, and for several gifts we offer detailed instructions.

Whatever your personal style, you'll find original and merry ways of expressing it here. I hope this book will inspire a Christmas as glad in the decorating as in the celebrating.

—*Nancy Lindemeyer*
Editor in Chief, Victoria *Magazine*

WHITE WINTER'S EVE

Conjure the season's radiance with white decorations and a sublime dinner—
and make your home as splendid as an evening brushed by angels' wings.

EVEN WHEN THE VIEW BEYOND THE WINDOW IS OF PALM TREES

or city spires, there's no reason not to enjoy a white Christmas. Few of us spend the holiday in the

dreamy landscape of a Christmas card, where deer might pick their way through pure drifts of

snow—although the tree in the living room may have been shipped from just such a place. But as

we trim the boughs, our imaginations fill with visions of snow and stars and angels.

For bringing that ethereal mood to a house or an apartment, no color is as magically effective

as white. Despite its arctic associations, white can be warming, for it captures sunlight and

brightens the shadows. Under white's spell, small spaces seem larger, greenery greener. And

however lavishly you adorn your rooms, nothing will seem overdone or cluttered. White has a

Romantic ruffles of fabric, such as a chair-seat cover (opposite), elevate the dreamy mood of a white Christmas. An angel ornament (above) looks most heavenly in a billowy organdy dress and little wings of ribbon.

unifying quality, just like those fleecy blankets of snow laid across rooftops, fields, and trees.

White Christmas! What a wonderful idea for a party. It's the perfect theme for a Yuletide bridal shower or wedding, of course, but why not organize a small tree-trimming party to which everyone brings a white ornament? Ask your guests to wear winter white. Prepare a crackling fire, a warm roasted dinner, fluffy desserts (see pages 23–27)—and, yes, a home transformed into a creamy confection itself.

Don't be tentative with white. Use it assertively in rich combinations of textures and materials. You may even find some makings at hand: bisque figurines, a mohair throw from the bedroom, a creamware pitcher to fill with white birch twigs. The effort needn't be costly. One family trims a little tabletop tree entirely with sun-bleached scallop shells gathered at the seashore. A collector of flea-market laces folds her finds into blossoms to tuck into a wreath. With ethereal and playful touches like these indoors, who cares if it doesn't snow?

Should a certain old gent drop in from the North Pole, he'd feel right at home in the snowy sparkle of this room. On the lustrous tree (opposite), sprinkled from tip to gifts with frosty treasures, are streamers of diaphanous organdy ribbon that lend a breezy motion to the boughs. Greet guests—or Santa—with a sideboard arrayed in silver (above) and laden with goodies for later. Hung from a mantel installed over an improvised candlelight "fireplace" (right) are stockings stitched from vintage Marseilles spreads and from damask and eyelet fabrics.

How to achieve a joyous sense of abundance without scatter and clutter? For excellence in a supporting role, clear glass containers surely get the decorators' award. Lidded candy jars (left) are filled with generous scoops of mints and silvery sugared almonds; urn-shaped apothecary jars (below) transform blown-glass ornaments into fairy-tale sweets. Group any and every shape of clear vessel—vases, brandy snifters, and compotes work just as well. Try filling them with shells, white-painted pinecones, or frosted cookies. Also behind glass, the shelves of a white cabinet (opposite) wink with unexpected delights: Each tier bubbles and sparkles with its own selection of glass ornaments from Germany. Perfectly placed atop the cabinet, the trio of apothecary jars serve as gleaming impromptu finials.

"Wassail, Wassail, all over the town! / Our toast it is white and our ale it is brown. / Our bowl it is made of the white maple tree; / With the wassailing bowl, we'll drink to thee."

—*The Gloucestershire Wassail*

an emphasis on white flowers

While the cutting garden slumbers in winter, fresh flowers are a store-bought miracle. But instead of the usual red poinsettias, try the pure dazzle of white blossoms.

✺ "Lo, like a rose e'er blooming," go the words of a German carol—and what could be more eloquent than a mantel of greenery (opposite) graced with ivory roses? To keep flowers looking their best in garlands or wreaths, tuck their freshly cut stems into water-filled florist's tubes and bury the little containers in the greenery.

✺ Snowy blossoms make a double impact in a container of the same color, such as a milk-glass vase or a creamware bowl. Look around the house for unexpected containers, too, like a folk-art clothespin basket (top right). Baskets can be made watertight with a plastic insert. An opaque container, whether a wooden box or a metal urn, has the advantage of hiding florist's foam—which not only holds water but also anchors stems for a secure arrangement.

✺ Florists have amazing selections, even in freezing weather: roses, lilies, calla lilies, and carnations, certainly, but you may also find amaryllis, stock, hellebores, freesia, statice, narcissus, and sweet peas. Try mixing complementary forms, such as the pointy petals of lilies (right) highlighted against shadows of arching juniper sprigs.

To make a gift garbed in white look as lovely as a wedding cake, tie a tiny bouquet of milliner's flowers (opposite), or of fresh flowers slipped in a florist's tube, into a bow of gossamer ribbon. An added ornament, like a little glass bird, will certainly stir fond memories during future tree trimmings.

KEEPSAKE GIFT BOXES *It hardly matters whether the contents of a wallpaper-covered bandbox (left) are a humble scarf or a pair of mittens. A fancy bandbox is a lovely gift in itself. Long ago, bandboxes were usually made at home; today, still, with glue and sturdy decorative paper, any cardboard box can be turned into attractive storage for everything from hats to magazine clippings to craft supplies. Knot a key-shaped ornament—or a big old-fashioned door key from a flea market—into the ribbons to suggest the promise of a secret inside.*

LAVENDAR-AND-CEDAR SACHET
A gift and its wrapping can be one in the same: A square of tulle (right) is gathered around a handful of dried lavender and other soothing herbs and tied into a bundle. Slipped into the ribbon bow is a nosegay of cedar and lavender—one so fragrant you'll want to pin it right onto your lapel. Such crisp snippets, which might be lost on colorfully patterned gift wrap, stand out against white like dapper boutonnieres.

Roasted meats have been the centerpiece of Christmas feasting since late-medieval times, when, to the fanfare of trumpets, servers marched into the great hall bearing platters of boar's head, venison, birds, and beef. Roasting marvelously concentrates the flavors, not just of meat but of vegetables and fruits as well, especially those available in autumn and winter. Perhaps best of all, while the oven does the work, you have more time to spend with your guests.

A WINTER'S EVE MENU: Maple-Glazed Roasted Duckling with Apples ❧ Sweet-and-Sour Roasted Beets ❧ Roasted Carrots with Ginger ❧ For dessert, choose one of our five light-as-a-cloud confections (following pages), all of which can be made ahead of time.

❧ Duck is a wonderful treat for a holiday dinner. The golden bird (above) is glazed with a soy-mustard sauce that crisps the skin and flavors sliced apples that are baked in the same pan. One farm-raised duck serves four, but it's no harder to roast two—just allow more time. To reduce fat, prick the skin all over and roast at a higher temperature for the first half hour. For the recipe, see page 112.

❧ Beets are to boil—or so most of us think. Not at all, believes Georgia Downard, *Victoria's* recipe tester, who planned this meal. Roast them whole, peel, cut into wedges, toss in a vinegar-honey sauce, and garnish with fresh dill (top left). What could be more festively red-and-green on the plate? For the recipe, see page 113.

❧ The carrots served with our meal (left) retain all their sweetness when roasted quickly—just twenty minutes at 450°F—with butter and freshly grated ginger. An orange-ginger-honey sauce and a sprinkling of minced fresh cilantro add zing. For the recipe, see page 113.

EGGS IN SNOW *The French call this dessert* oeufs à la neige; *it is also known as* île flottante, *or "floating island." Thomas Jefferson introduced it to America in 1789, after his sojourn in Paris. In our version (right), fresh ginger infuses the poached meringue "eggs" as well as the custard sauce they float on. Julienned strips of chewy candied ginger garnish the meringues. For the most traditional presentation, choose a wide soup plate, and don't forget a soup spoon.* *Turn to page 114 for the recipe.*

FILLED MERINGUE SHELLS
Meringue shells, whether brimming with berries and whipped cream or with scoops of colorful sorbets and ice creams, are irresistible to young and old alike. Ours (left) hold raspberries nestled beneath a piped swirl of Chantilly cream subtlely flavored with rose water. To emphasize the floral essense, each dessert is sprinkled with a cascade of edible rose petals. *The recipe is on page 115.*

ALMOND BAVARIAN WITH POACHED PEARS *As with our other beautiful finales, almond-infused Bavarian creams (opposite) can be made ahead of time. Little clouds of flavor, they're based on a rich classic but done with a lighter, brighter touch. The individually molded Bavarians are haloed by slices of poached pears; then, for a pleasing trio of textures, they are sprinkled with toasted slivered almonds.* *See page 116 for the recipe.*

COCONUT ANGEL FOOD CAKES *There's no lighter cake to bite into than angel food (opposite), certainly appropriate during Christmas. And when each serving is baked in an individual cake mold, every guest gets more of that chewy golden outside. What lifts this version up into the empyrean is a glaze of sweetened coconut milk topped with crunchy flakes of grated coconut. For the recipe, see page 117.*

WHITE-CHOCOLATE MOUSSE *For dramatic effect, serve each portion of this silky white-chocolate mousse (right), in a tall wine goblet, and top with shavings of white chocolate— use a vegetable peeler to make the curls. Add a crisp cookie for the ideal contrast of textures. For the recipe, turn to page 118.*

"At Christmas be mery, and thanke God of all:
and feast thy pore neighbors, the great and the small."

—*Thomas Tusser, 1577*

chapter two

HEIRLOOM CHRISTMAS

No other holiday connects us so deeply to our past through beloved family treasures—and offers such a promise-filled chance to build our own collections.

HERE IT IS, THE SOFTLY WORN GLASS BIRD GRANDMOTHER brought from Germany and, deeper in the box, that tiny china cradle Sister presented the year the first baby arrived. One is an antique, the other is not, but both speak of many Christmas seasons.

Whether our ornaments and decorations are inherited or bought, memories are what we hang each year on the evergreen's boughs. The little Nutcracker figure carried home from a trip abroad, the pinecones gathered at a friend's farm—they return to tell their stories, and make collectors of us all.

Now, more than ever, is the time to unpack and polish that prized but seldom-used silver punch bowl and fill it, if not with punch, then with glass balls and fresh greenery. Or unfold the damask tablecloth, packed away in tissue since Thanksgiving, and reveal a great-aunt's monogram.

The legend of The Nutcracker *holds that beloved toys come alive at Christmas. Encourage the magic by inviting beautiful playthings of long ago (opposite) or even a floppy-eared pup from childhood (above) to join the festivities.*

> "I made four gilt stars for the four top branches, and Ma dressed a little doll like a fairy in white with spangles."
>
> —*Harriet Beecher Stowe, 1850*

The chance to put treasured heirlooms unabashedly on display is part of what makes the holidays so festive and meaningful.

Our very best heirlooms, though, are the happy memories themselves. So delight homecoming adult children with toys saved from their childhoods—even that funny Styrofoam ball made in kindergarten, adorned with more gluey fingerprints than ribbon. Or frame a daughter's first poem (of course you kept it) in a little wreath; she might be pleased to learn that penned verses ornamented some of the very earliest American Christmas trees.

Odd collections you hadn't thought of as "Christmassy"—faded vacation postcards, even toy cars or a doll's tea cups—can, with a bit of thread attached, turn a plain wreath or banister garland into a family story. And why not crowd the boughs of a child's own little tree with Steiff bears or Beanie Babies wearing red-ribbon bows? However whimsical the items, it is the grouping that makes the impact.

When a holiday is filled with such joyous symbols as stars, angels, music, and the gentle animals of the manger, who can resist becoming a collector? One family celebrates its musical

A tabletop tree (above) can become a holiday display cabinet for antique toys, trinkets, and family photos. But mixing treasures and greenery need not stop at the tree. A doorstop cast as a sheep and lamb (right) greets guests in a merry collar of greens; paintings (opposite) become the grandest of all ornaments when crowned with lush plumes of greenery.

talents by gathering toy instruments for its tree; another fills the house with magical stars and moons in every material, from glass to paper to gilded wood. These collectors are eternally on the hunt: In their eyes, a piece of rummage-sale costume jewelry or a decorative curtain tieback can easily join the parade of Christmas ornaments. Before long, friends and family invariably catch the spirit, swelling the collections with their own gifts.

Count yourself lucky if your Christmas box contains a sewn and stuffed cotton apple crafted by a nineteenth-century American child or a paper cornucopia ornamented with a Victorian chromolithograph and wired tinsel. Antique and vintage ornaments have become valuable and sought-after collector's items today. But be on the watch at florist's shops and local craft fairs: Perhaps you'll discover an artisan whose creations captivate you. If so, you've found your Christmas heirlooms of tomorrow.

What speaks of your past? In the Tennessee home of fashion designer Pat Kerr, chubby celluloid Santas (opposite and above right) hold pride of place on an antique hand-carved mantel. "These were dime-store items when I was a child. In those days, the five-and-ten seemed like a Christmas wonderland," says Pat, who avidly collects these vintage Saint Nicks and insists that "each has a distinct personality." Memories of more formal decorations are conjured by her grandmother's silver chalice and bowls (right), brought forth for the season and made even more reflective with handfuls of gleaming balls.

RIBBON STAR AND GARLAND

Ribbon can be coaxed into more than bows. To make a luxurious garland (left), tie the ends of three spooled ribbons together, then braid, unrolling as you go along. The star ornament, whose shape is borrowed from a 1920s hat cockade, is made by folding ribbon and stitching it to a disk of buckram. See pages 130–31 to learn how to make it.

BUTTON-HEART ORNAMENTS

Be as sentimental or original as you like with these homemade baubles (right). To learn how to make one, turn to page 132.

CANDLESTICK MANTELSCAPE

A tightly grouped array of mismatched candlesticks sings a lovely carol on any holiday mantel. This all-brass procession (opposite) harmonizes with a mix of gold and white tapers.

CHANDELIER ORNAMENT DROPS

The holidays are a shining hour for chandeliers. Twine the arms with translucent ribbon and long-lasting leaves, such as eucalyptus (opposite) or bay laurel; using fishing line or colored cord, suspend large glass balls to softly reflect the light. Experiment with different themes, perhaps hanging vintage glittered pinecones or tinsel and translucent glass icicles. A chandelier so adorned would be as fitting a decoration for a New Year's Eve party as it would be for Christmas dinner.

SETTING THE MANTEL AGLIMMER

Instead of decorating the mantel with the familiar bold reds and forest greens, try blending more subtle hues: the gleam of silver and glass, the frosty greens of olive leaves and seeded eucalyptus (above and left). Slender blown-glass candlesticks make elegant pedestals for shiny and frosty orbs, echoed by more ornaments dancing beneath the under-mantel swag. Beaded votives, tiny wrapped gifts, oversize mercury-glass balls, gauzy ribbon—whatever plays into your scheme will add interest. Though this is an opulent, crowded mantel, it appears as one balanced whole—and the motif can be carried throughout the room or throughout the entire house.

Bejeweled Curtain Tiebacks

Rich brocades seem made for festivities. A dramatic and especially simple way to use them is to sew holiday tiebacks (opposite) for the curtains. Use fabric or wide ribbon that coordinates with existing curtains and adds a bold sweep of luxury. Give them glamour by either hooking or basting on tiny ornaments. The leaves that top these red balls are not just pretty; they also disguise the point of attachment.

"Let every house be ready tonight, / The children gathered, the candles alight, / That music to hear, to see that sight."

—*P. Cornelius, German carol*

Chairs in Their Holiday Best

For a formal dinner, make guests feel like royalty by dressing the dining chairs in sumptuous fabric. The effort involved in making loose-fitting slipcovers will be repaid as you use them to decorate year after year. For a flowing, capelike silhouette (right), add a box pleat to the back. Each year, dress up the chair back differently by pinning on a cluster of balls and gilded leaves (above) or a tassel of pinecones tied with a silk cord or a ribbon bow.

Ornamented Table Settings

As an ornament collection grows too large for the tree, look for more places to direct the overflow. For a long-lasting centerpiece (right), mound ornaments in a footed compote, and lace with sprigs of leaves and berries. If it sits on a table against a wall, tuck in a short strand of tiny lights. Dangling from a candelabrum (opposite), tiny balls seem to float above a table already festooned with ornaments. Instead of place cards, use monogrammed Christmas balls: Write the initial of each guest with a gold glitter pen, or paint each letter with a fine brush and craft glue; then, working over a bowl to catch the excess, sprinkle with fine-grained glitter.

embroidery for gifts

In time-honored tradition, needle and thread are all that you need to personalize a handmade gift or embellish a store-bought one.

∾ A wreath of ribbons embroidered with the monograms of many family members and friends (opposite) was a popular sentimental remembrance of weddings or reunions in the nineteenth century. Today, such a wreath would make a thoughtful tribute to a family matriarch. To learn how to make one, turn to page 133.

∾ Practical gifts of winter clothing for children may be in need of extra charm. This woolen pocket (right) was machine-embroidered; a similar design could be done by hand. Simpler enhancements are felt patches (below), which can be easily whipstitched to a scarf or hat.

GIFT SACKS AND SACHETS

It's hard to part with a favorite chintz slipcover worn beyond repair or a gaily printed forties kitchen tablecloth that has more holes than folds. Salvage intact portions for making a gift sack or sachet (left): Cut a rectangle of fabric whose length is at least three times its width. Turn the short ends under $1/4$ inch—twice, if desired— and hem, or leave the ends raw if you're making many little sacks for party favors. Fold in the middle, with right sides facing, and sew the two outside edges, leaving the short end open. Turn right side out, fill with a gift or with a scoop of your favorite sachet blend, and tie the bundle closed with a pretty ribbon.

TABLETOP RIBBON SCREEN

Far prettier than any bulletin board, a small fabric-covered screen (opposite) can hold postcards, snapshots, poems, or Christmas cards in its taut lattice of ribbons. When not in use, it folds for easy storage—or for easy wrapping as a gift. See pages 134–135 for instructions.

CLOSET FINDS

Many of us have bits of fabric and ribbon tucked away that we mean to use—a torn vintage quilt, lace trim intended for curtains never made. There lies potential: Lace ribbon hangs a ball more prettily than wire (right); a quilt that's had its day can be cut down to cover a desk-chair cushion or turn a blanket-chest lid into a soft, cozy seat.

paper mementos

Generations past were dedicated collectors of paper ephemera. Magazines, cards, and colored chromolithographs were all carefully tucked away, one day to be pasted in albums or used at Christmas. Many a family sat at the kitchen table with scissors, glue, and tinsel wire late into the night, making ornaments and decoupaged gifts.

∽ To make a traveler's memory box (opposite)—for ticket stubs, journals, or letters from home—decoupage a plain wooden box from a crafts-supply store with old maps and prints of far-off places.

∽ Vintage cards and old photos (below) can be affixed with glue to journal covers or even to a candle's glass cylinder (right). Consider an item's value before cutting or gluing—perhaps use a color photocopy.

chapter three

A GARDENER'S HOLIDAY

*While one garden sleeps, another may bloom indoors. So go a-gathering—
boughs and pods and bulbs and berries await to fill your home.*

A FEW DRIED STALKS ARCH OVER THE SNOW THAT
blankets the garden; even the thick pines shiver in the wind. For gardeners, impatient for the season

of growth, winter is a time of yearning, no matter how many colorful catalogs they pore over.

But for *Victoria*'s garden editor, Tovah Martin, the holidays are a gleeful time, a chance to fill the

house to the rafters with nature's gifts. A wheelbarrow full of fresh greens of all varieties keeps cool

on the porch of her Connecticut house; the bulbs she's coaxed awake are moved to the windowsills.

Baskets of pinecones, fruits, and mosses stand ready to deck the halls in whatever ways her

imagination devises. "Just smelling them, working with them, makes me happy," says Tovah. "I find

I have too much fun decorating to remember to miss the garden."

*Wreaths hung on porch
posts (opposite) issue
a jaunty invitation
when positioned at
different heights. Cut
paper-whites and
snips of greenery in a
vintage tiered flower
pot (above) serve as
a sweet-scented beacon
in a frosty window.*

The two high "standards" on a Victorian-style plant stand (above) didn't take years of training or come from an expensive florist. The result of a moment's inspiration, they're made of half-stripped cuttings from a hedge. Once the stems were braided and wired together, leaving the tops bushy, they were "planted" in floral foam that was waiting in the waterproof boxes.

"I'm not one for a lot of glitter and tinsel at Christmastime," admits Tovah, who spent many years working in a family greenhouse and nursery and, like gardeners everywhere, longs to have green things around her all through the winter. Her country house, part of which is a remodeled barn, seems as suited to nature's aesthetics as Tovah herself is. Yet plant materials used abundantly, she points out, can be just as eloquent in a city apartment or a suburban home—and a lovely way of honoring the earth in this sacred season.

Half the fun of decorating this way is playing hunter-gatherer. Depending on your region, there's much that can be gleaned on a walk through your yard or a country lane where gathering is permitted—perhaps hemlock, spruce, silky white pine, the silvery pods of milkweed, red barberries, or glistening rose hips. Right around the house may be box, ivy, privet, or the budded branches of andromeda. City foragers can have luck, too: Often you can pick up the sawed-off branches at Christmas-tree lots for free. Then look to the fruit stand or farmers' market for color: pomegranates, pink-cheeked lady apples, green Granny Smith apples, even white eggplants—all are like paints for an artist of nature.

"I also plan ahead," says Tovah. "I save up wire baskets to stuff with moss, and raffia for tying branches together. And whenever I go for a walk, I fill my pockets with pinecones."

When Tovah's friend, North Carolina florist Karen Caubel, arrived for the holidays with a carful of arborvitae, silvery acacia, and

Although the barn's big living room (above) isn't strictly in the rustic style of furnishing, every corner has its country-grown surprise. On the mantel, scattered seed pods and greens, framed by potted rosemary, seem to tumble out of a still-life painting. Behind the Wardian case—a small indoor greenhouse that was all the rage in nineteenth-century parlors—Tovah centered a sizable wreath on each tall window (left); a tiny wreath hangs on the front of the case itself.

> "Children love building their own arrangements with whatever greens or berries are at hand—because you can't go wrong."
>
> —*Floral designer Karen Caubel*

Flowers and greenery are gorgeous in profusion, no matter the scale. A garden-inspired tree (opposite) gets its breathtaking lushness from tucked-in branches of additional foliage. A miniature wire basket (above) is lined with sphagnum moss and water-soaked floral foam before its tight little bouquet is assembled.

big bunches of roses, the two women happily snipped and chatted for days, strewing the floor with petals and stems as they decorated the house together. "We made a Christmas 'tree of trees,'" says Tovah, "by plumping out the boughs with guest greenery"—rosemary bunches here, some acacia there, a burst of white baby's breath, a cluster of lichen—giving the tree as much visual variety as any collection of shiny glass ornaments.

Pots of all sorts were lined up on the windowsill, including forced paper-whites and a huge amaryllis with red-streaked blossoms. With the help of a wire form, trailing ivy was wound into a wreath. "More!" cried Tovah as she squeezed her little pot of chives from the kitchen in among the rest.

Karen, meanwhile, acting secretively, had turned to filling little wire baskets. "Don't watch right now," she warned her friend. "I'm hiding your presents inside them." But since the baskets—bursting with roses, berries, and greenery (wonderful on a dining or coffee table)—looked like gifts themselves, the two filled tiny wire ones, each different, to hang on the tree and give to visiting friends.

f o r c e d - b u l b   g i f t s   a n d   d e c o r a t i o n s

It's hard to imagine a sight more cheering in winter than trumpets of spring flowers, perhaps in a massed display like the one shown below. These are living bouquet gifts, perfect for hostess, friend, or neighbor. And an attractive, reusable container is part of the gift; a gardener impatient for spring might also enjoy beribboned tools, as shown opposite. The trick with forcing is to plan ahead, calculating backward from when you want to see the flowers. Books and garden centers can provide information on forcing many kinds of bulbs; here are a few ideas.

Fragrant paper-white narcissus are the easiest bulbs to force because they don't require a period of chilling to form roots. In a well-drained pot with two inches of soil or a watertight container with two inches of gravel, cluster the bulbs closely, then add more soil or gravel, up to the bulbs' shoulders. If you use soil, keep it moist; in gravel, keep water just touching the bottoms of the bulbs. Keep the container in a sunny spot and watch spring happen early—in six to eight weeks.

Hyacinths, large-flowering crocuses, muscari, miniature *Iris reticulata*, and miniature daffodils need to believe they've had their winter's beauty sleep. They must rest and root for about twelve weeks after potting in a cold, but not freezing, place, such as a garage or a refrigerator. Keep them slightly moist; when green blades nose up, bring them out for forcing, which takes another three weeks. If they're budding too early, slow the process by moving pots to a cooler, darker place for a while.

POMANDER AND BOXWOOD TREE

The kitchen, where we spend so much time during the holidays, deserves its own touches of gladness. To create a fragrant countertop tree (right), first dot oranges with whole cloves in swirled or striped patterns. Attach them to a floral-foam cone with toothpicks or snips of bamboo skewers, then fill the remainder of the cone with sprigs of boxwood or other greenery— floral picks may make the job easier. For more color, add a string of dried cranberries.

FRAGRANT KITCHEN WINDOWS

Who can resist the scent of spices and herbs in the air? Use them for decorating—as well as cooking—in the kitchen. Dried apple slices and cinnamon sticks tied with raffia (left) make a countertop window as lovely to look at as it is to gaze through. On Christmas Day, free all those herbs from the refrigerator—set them out in jars, and enjoy their aromas and textures.

PATTERNED ORANGE POMANDERS

We've all learned to stud an orange all over with whole cloves, grateful for their pointy, stubby stems. But "all over" is just one possible pattern for a pomander. Using a citrus stripper, carve radiating spokes (opposite), cascading swirls, or a cross-hatched harlequin pattern into the fruit's rind; then insert cloves until you're satisfied with the design. Add a plume of fluffy pine to make a jolly decoration for a special friend.

birds in winter

A quaint birdhouse covered in snow, perhaps a tiny wreath hung at its peak—this is sure to bring us a smile on a winter walk in the garden. Here are a few ways to thank the birds themselves.

Make a suet ball. Save bacon or other meat fats, or use lard. Chill the fat, then combine thoroughly with mixed birdseed. Knot a loop of string for hanging and enmesh it in the mixture as you form the suet into a ball. Wrap in plastic and freeze. Hang it from a branch near a window, then watch the birds gather and feast.

To attract the royal flash of the cardinal, scatter birdseed on the ground—the females, especially, are shy of bird feeders. Sunflower seeds, with their high fat content, are appealing to most birds.

c h a p t e r   f o u r

TEA PARTY IN
PASTELS

*Turn an afternoon gathering into a fete with a setting inspired by the rosy blush
of sugarplums. And don't scrimp on the real sweets.*

THERE'S NO MORE EXCITING TIME OF YEAR TO ENTERTAIN

than during the holidays, when families and friends reunite. Students and young married couples

return to hearth and home; there are new babies to celebrate, old ties to renew. Now the spicy aroma

of baking cookies and the scent of pine boughs fill the house. The scene is set for a party.

Often, that sweet lull between Christmas and New Year's finds everyone most relaxed and available,

so choose one of those frequently overlooked days. An afternoon tea party is ideal for including all

ages, from indulgent grandfathers to little girls who will delight in nibbling sweets and showing off

their party dresses. And whether it's an open house or a celebration in a special someone's honor,

you'll have every excuse to orchestrate a welcoming wonderland. Given the general razzle-dazzle

*Two trees double the
magic: As a center-
piece on the tea table
(opposite), a little
evergreen is the
decorative echo of the
parlor's big tree. Both
trees display sugar-
paste ornaments, like
this fancy fan (above),
fit for a princess.*

"Now Christmas is come, let's beat up the drum, and call all our neighbors together."

—*Washington Irving*

of Christmas, soft pastels are a soothing and elegant theme. Think of the colors of petit fours, peonies, faded chintz. It's an unexpected palette, but Christmas is all about surprises.

And what better chance to delight in pretty confections than over tea? Bite-size treats, such as tiny meringues, strawberries, truffles, lemon squares, chocolate macaroons—and, of course, tea sandwiches—are easy for guests to manage. Good tea, punch for the children, perhaps a pot of chocolate, and some sherry and port will keep the party rolling merrily. By then, the sun will have set, candles will be aglow, and everyone will be too replete even to think of supper.

Sweets in homemade cones or baskets were hung on the earliest American Christmas trees. Expanding lavishly on that tradition, an enticing tree (opposite) blossoms with flowers, fans, and a cupid-painted "hand mirror" (above), all made of sugar by a master confectioner. Even the blown-glass Santa (right) recalls a molded chocolate in a candy cup. For a similar effect, a tree could be adorned with silk flowers, paper fans, tissue-wrapped favors, and cookies piped with pink and white royal icing.

Whatever you serve your guests at holiday time, present it with a flourish. A tiered stand (opposite) is improvised by stacking a silver cake basket atop a plate and encircling it with sugar-paste roses. And remember that family members, too, deserve the best. When Mother arrives, weary from traveling, or your sweetheart is up late wrapping presents, a beautiful offering, such as a pot of hot chocolate and a Linzer torte cookie (above), is more than a pick-me-up; it's a message of love. Even pierced creamware (right) can be made prettier with a narrow ribbon slipped through the rim and finished in a bow.

During winter's short afternoons, candles may gleam at teatime. In an unexpected pairing, pale pink roses mingle with blushing turnips on a tiered ceramic center-piece (opposite). Be sure to position the votives so they clear the plate above them.

GLASS-COMPOTE
LUSTER *A faceted glass compote reflects and refracts the light of floating candles (left), mimicking the effect of an antique crystal luster. Two look grand on a sideboard; one, with gently scented candles, is a calming touch on a nightstand.*

BUNDLED
CANDLE GIFTS

Favors of beeswax candles (right) send guests home with a glow. Wrap a pillar or a pair of tapers with lengths of pretty paper or fabric—torn edges, as shown, have a romantic appeal; bind with ribbon, then seal with stamped wax.

using antique linens

Beautiful linens often remain stowed away—either they're precious heirlooms or damaged treasures. Here are ways to liberate them.

✍ Hang beautiful antique garments, such as an exquisite christening gown and cap (right), on the wall. As with art, keep them out of direct sunlight. What a delightful, soft touch for a guest room!

✍ Sew pretty fragments of lace or embroidery into whimsically shaped ornaments (below). Stuff each like a pin-cushion, and add a loop for hanging. Worn or stained matelassé coverlets (opposite) can be cut down and reborn as bureau scarves, café curtains, or pillow shams. Our thrifty great grandmothers would be proud!

WHIMSY
IN THE SNOW

*Wood sprites and elves, draw near. Here's a Christmas frolic for the artist
in us all, born of materials simple, natural, and close at hand.*

GROWN-UPS ARE OFTEN MUCH TOO PREOCCUPIED AT HOLIDAY

time to pray for a snowstorm. But children wish for one so fervently and continuously that

sometimes it actually happens. When the yard is blanketed in whiteness, and trees stand robed like

heroes and heroines, grown-ups remember what it was to be a child, at play in the amazing, natural world.

Among the adults who have never put aside that feeling are artists. One of those artists, Sarah

Lugg, who lives in England, created the fanciful outdoor Christmas scene on these pages to show

us what a free and playful spirit can do to express the wonderment of the season. In Sarah's hands,

a feather, a leaf, a shell—the sorts of things you bring home in your pocket from a walk—become

gift tags and ornaments. Twigs turn into hearts, tinfoil into birds. "I just can't help saving things,"

*A fantastical outdoor
tree (opposite) wears
ornaments crafted from
ferns and feathers
and other snippets by
artist Sarah Lugg.
So tiny is the snowman
visiting this scene
(above) that he needs
only a few holly leaves
for his jaunty hat.*

"Good King Wenceslas looked out / On the Feast of Stephen, / When the snow lay round about, / Deep and crisp and even."
—*John Mason Neale, 1853 carol*

For a party table in tune with the winter land-scape, mismatched creamware plates (above) have both purity of color and variety of pattern. Shapely porcelain pears, adorned with hand-snipped tinfoil oak leaves, decorate each place and build on the theme. When friends are coming, there's no reason that relaxed, rustic elements like these country-style chairs and blankets used as tablecloths (opposite) can't keep company with china and sparkling crystal.

says Sarah, "and I have since I was a child—buttons, dried rosebuds, old stamps, colored beach glass. Their textures and origins speak to me. And I've learned through using them in my art that they speak to others as well."

When imagination quickens at Christmas, many of us entertain childhood's flickering fantasies. What if we invited the birds to break-fast? What if we could walk right into a Christmas card? What if, instead of bringing greenery inside, we brought everything outside? It takes an artist to follow through on such high-flying what-ifs, to create what the rest of us dream. So Sarah transported all the elements of a magical dinner party out into the snowy field—which, it turns out, made its own suggestions. "White cloths," it said clearly. "Icy crystal."

For a midwinter fete, you, too, might listen to the field and set a table of snowiest napery, layering several different cloths—or throws or blankets—to run the table's length. There must be candles, certainly, but sheltered from the wind in hurricanes. Play with white textures: alabaster and marble, creamware, shimmering shells. That's how Sarah thought. "I wanted a

shivery, glimmering effect for the table," she says. It so happened that all these ideas, including the little wrapped present left on each chair, were waiting for her family guests on Christmas Eve. "But we dined indoors, of course," she adds sensibly.

Like many of us, Sarah Lugg started creating handmade ornaments when she was a child. Unlike most of us, however, she never stopped, and she's compelled to try something new every year. Some of the same tools and materials she used as a girl are in her studio today: scissors, glue, stencils, thin wire, ribbon, beads, yarn, and all sorts of paper, from ornately printed tissues that once wrapped Italian chocolates to faded handwritten letters. Every once in a while, her husband, Robert, will come across one of her little hoards and ask, "Sarah, is this rubbish or is it art?"

It's art when you make it so. If postage stamps become a heart, or tin takes wings, or shells gleam with gold paint, or red buttons spell out "Be Merry" on a wide ribbon, then, yes, it's art. Moreover, the tree you adorn or the kitchen window you gladden are entirely, individually yours, not assembled from standard-issue items snatched up from a store. Inventing decorations from simple, found materials also connects us to quieter Yuletides of the past, for our ancestors did the same, filling the evenings with invention and expectation. "Play Christmas music while you work," advises Sarah Lugg. "It helps."

As if convention had taken flight, a layered centerpiece (above) refuses to stop at the lovely pierced cream-ware urn brimming with white flowers. Grasses and branches, whispy alternatives to greenery, etch the air and hold afloat a silvery message. Using a utility knife, Sarah traced the letters on heavy-gauge foil; she attached them with thin silver wire to keep them from twirling.

The heart—a symbol of love, hope, and joy—is as welcome at Christmas as on Valentine's Day. A heart-shaped twig wreath hung on each chair (left) welcomes guests to the table; tags inscribed with everyone's initials organize the seating. Strung at the frosty windows (above left) are treats for the children: shortbread cookies in glassine envelopes, numbered for each day of Advent with glued-on daisies, mother-of-pearl buttons, and button-head mums, and finished with vintage gold bullion stars. Substitute monograms for numbers on the bags, and use them as place cards. Among the many different hearts on the tree is a collage of stamps, its edges aged by singeing before being glued to the tag.

g i f t w r a p s   f r o m   n a t u r e

At the end of December, the seconds of day-light are gaining, a cause for celebration in ancient times, long before the first Christmas. Embellish each present's wrapping with reminders of the earth's gifts, coordinating the colors, themes, and materials with the decoration of the tree, as shown opposite.

∽ A container worth keeping, such as this lidded basket (top right), doubles the pleasure of a gift, regardless of what waits within. Small wooden boxes, a hand-made cone of natural paper or bark, even an unbleached linen tea towel tied nicely becomes a gift holding a gift.

∽ You needn't sign "Love" when the wrapping says it clearly. Sarah not only dripped a wax heart onto her card (center right), she added the kiss of a dried dogwoood blossom and rosebud. Look for ribbons, cords, and trimmings like this giant rickrack, which complement the colors and textures of your natural accents.

∽ A snippet of preserved fern frond mounted on a manila tag (bottom right) forms the silhouette of a Christmas tree in miniature. A wee box of fudge waiting at each guest's place carries the innocently artful tag. "Leaves," notes Sarah, "are often more exquisitely shaped than flowers."

BUTTONED STARFISH ORNAMENT *One star in the East, many in the sea: Bejewel a starfish with pearly buttons of similar size (left), using dabs of quick-drying glue. Any all-white ornament of graphic shape shows up vividly against green boughs.*

DRESSED-UP STOCKINGS *Individualize plain stockings, such as these shimmering ice-blue ones (opposite), with cuffs of luxurious ruffle, pleats, or jeweled ribbon found at fabric or trimmings shops. Tie on a shell or feather for a natural touch.*

SARAH'S DOVE OF PEACE *Or is it an angel in flight? Cut from heavy-gauge aluminum foil, these tiny messengers can be adorned with gold paint to highlight feathers and beaks. "I made one carrying a gold heart," said Sarah. "An olive branch was too tricky."*

m a k i n g   t a g   o r n a m e n t s

Often, in her poster art, Sarah arranges rhythmic rows of ornamented light-brown tags. "But for the tree (below), white tags show
best," she advises. Buy tags in quantity at stationery stores. Then
the fun begins. Choose a shape (such as a heart), a color scheme
(perhaps pink and red), or an idea (such as "the beach"), and play.

✑ A pressed fern frond (opposite left) is anchored with dabs of
glue. To make a dried-rosebud heart (opposite right), lightly draw
the shape on the tag, paint the shape with glue, then carefully
position buds, one by one. Let the card dry flat and undisturbed.

✑ Two red feathers, crossed, unexpectedly become a heart (right);
they can be attached to the tag with staples or a bit of glue.

Light in darkness, a star in the sky—it's the very essence of Christmas. From solitary farmhouses to city blocks, we light the world in this season with bright reminders of hope. An outdoor tree can be more than a string or two of lights: While all the ornaments on Sarah's tree (opposite) shouldn't remain outdoors, a tree decorated with securely attached glass balls and icicles could stand in the yard through the season to greet all who pass by. When guests are expected, light their way to your door with candles set in windowed lanterns (right), which cast fluttering shadows—and the warmest of welcomes—on the cold drifts of winter.

"Unlatch the door at midnight /And let your lantern's glow/
Shine out to guide the traveler's feet / To you across the snow."

—Joyce Kilmer, "Gates and Doors"

chapter six

'TIS THE SILVER
SEASON

The world over, bells ring out for Christmas. Capture the gleam and the joy of that sterling peal with lustrous decorations, both subtle and sumptuous.

OUTSIDE, EVERY TWIG AND TREE IS GLAZED, FLASHING IN THE SUN.

Mother Nature's ice storm—a morning's magic—has left a shimmering world behind. But we, too,

have our own ways of shining. And one is to transform our homes with the holiday spirit of silver.

A poet once noted that there is no rhyme in English for the word *silver*. Still, decorations keyed

to this hue suggest a visual rhyme scheme, especially when linked with dove gray, pewter, and silky

white. Silver can be as reserved as a Paul Revere bowl, as merry as a tinkling bell. For those who feel

that less is more, silver ornaments, misty fabrics, and sage-hued greenery make a polished statement

in a soft voice. This is certainly the season to display fine heirloom pieces: One collector hangs

silver tea strainers on her tree. Another ties espresso spoons into a cedar window corsage.

An entry-hall tree (opposite) is elegant dressed in frosted cookies. Shaped as symbols of nature and as glass ornaments (above), the cookies were artfully adorned with tinted royal icing, sugar crystals, and silver dragées.

"Now Christmas comes, 'tis fit that we/Should feast and sing, and merry be/ Keep open House, let Fiddlers play/A Fig for Cold, sing Care away"

---Virginia Almanack, 1766

Your welcome begins at the front door with a proclamation that Christmas is in residence. Hang a spray of vines or birch twigs mingled with evergreen leaves, such as laurel or magnolia, and studded with silver sleigh bells. Indoors, fill your hall with seasonal aromas: balsam, spruce, orange-cinnamon potpourri, or similarly scented candles. Once your company is jingled indoors, greet them under a kissing ball made of boxwood snippets (a safe alternative to mistletoe) inserted into a floral-foam globe and hung from silver cord. It's an old—and enchantingly flirtatious—Yuletide tradition.

If the weather is temperate enough, flower arrangements can be moved outside to help usher visitors to the door. Three shapely painted garden urns (above) were fitted with watertight liners and floral foam, then filled with seeded eucalyptus and a ring of full-blown creamy white roses. The welcome should continue inside, of course, so why serve the eggnog from the dining-room sideboard so far away? A grand silver punch bowl set in the entry hall (right) lets guests share in the good cheer as soon as they arrive.

A graceful front-hall banister is a natural and long-favored place to hang a garland. Cedar forms the base of this garland (right), providing a dark, feathery backdrop for contrasting seed pods, greenery, and luscious blooms of white amaryllis at the top of the newel post. The serpentine drape doesn't just enhance the bottom step's curve; it points right to the hall's "centerpiece"— a proudly polished punch bowl and cups.

Silver that has been loved for generations gains a mellow patina, and many vintage or antique pieces survive for the observant collector to find—and use imaginatively. On a mantel (opposite), a pedigreed creamer, julep cup, and champagne bucket are treated casually as pedestals for pears and a myrtle topiary. Don't overlook the family baby cups; they, too, add sheen—and memories—to the display. Silver needn't have a past, however, or even be real, for that matter. The chrome paint that shines up pitted bicycle handles turned a bird cage (right) into a palace for flickering votives. For another sterling effect, fill silver containers, from vases to a tea caddy (below), with greenery, ornaments, and coils of silvery ribbon and cord too pretty to leave in the trimmings basket. This arrangement gleams beneath a crystal-drop girandole.

*Silver and gold enjoy a regal bond, so Christmas
is the perfect time to use them both on the table.
For couture-style drama, layer two tablecloths:
Golden plaid silk over Battenburg lace (opposite)
is gathered into a ribboned flounce. The best
gold-rimmed china and stemware (left) mix
sumptuously with silver chargers and flatware.
Even the sugared fruits of the centerpiece seem
frosted with silver dust. To make a little girl feel
like a true princess, use bead-embroidered
fabric to stitch a fancy-dress stocking (above left).
Carry out the look of luxury anywhere with
mounds of readily available silvered ornaments
(above), here atop a cushion of boxwood.*

keeping holiday journals

So much to do, so little time. Too often, seasonal rituals that should bring us pleasure seem like chores. The cure for a spinning mind is to retreat to a serene corner and get organized. Journals can help recapture the joy—and ease your efforts.

~ Keep a card journal. As you open this year's holiday cards, keep a list of those to whom you forgot to send your greetings. Add new friends to your list; note changed addresses before you toss out the envelopes, as well as new family status (the name of a new wife or baby). And what about those cherished annual letters from far-flung friends? Tape two journal pages together at the bottom and side to make a pocket. Rereading the letters will bring others close as you write next year's card.

~ Organize a family Christmas album. Your daughter hugging her first bicycle, Grandpa in his Santa hat—are all those wonderful photos piled in a forgotten shoebox? A special photo album with captions ("Matthew gets a backpack for his semester abroad") stitches a living thread from year to year. Whose was the funniest present? What was the greatest surprise? Bring out the album after the goose and finally resolve the debates.

Let the porch, the deck, the walkway join in the celebration. Not everyone owns an antique pony cart (opposite), but anything from a little red wagon to a yard cart or a weathered planter can over-flow with natural abundance. Combine textures and tones of silvers and grays played against subtle hues of green. This is also a beautiful way to keep materials for your indoor decorations fresh until you need them. An old sled painted white (left) is a cheerful backdrop for a pair of vintage skates and a bunch of seeded eucalyptus that seems to have been tied in a ribbon by Jack Frost himself; a window box behind the sled boasts a winter "planting" of more cut greenery.

"Gentle, at home, amid/My friends I'll be/
Like the high leaves/Upon the holly tree."

—*Godey's Lady's Book, 1890*

chapter seven

A GLORIOUS
GLOWING FEAST

It's the season for indulgent and lavish dining, as well as for the comfort of traditional fare. Bring both, beautifully, to your holiday table.

SPARKLING CRYSTAL, A FULLY SET TABLE, A WARMING FIRE.

Whether the occasion is a fancy Christmas dinner party for close friends or a feast on New Year's

Eve, make the table as celebratory as possible. But make the food, too, as felicitous as you can, for

food is the soul of the gathering. In planning such a special menu, many of us pore over cookbooks

for months, tempted to dazzle with new and complicated dishes. The opposite inclination is to fall

back on time-honored, foolproof favorites that, good as they are, hold few surprises. Is there a way

to delight and comfort at once, to strike a balance? Yes.

To simplify last-minute preparations, choose a first course that's cold yet luxurious, such as

oysters, crabmeat, gravlax, or pâté. Whatever the main dish, complementing it with a sauce

Even in an exuberant setting, like the dining room at the Hope and Glory Inn (opposite), little touches like wrapped favors, a pineapple carved into a candlestick, and small bouquets (above) bespeak a personal sense of hospitality.

Serving shellfish is something of a tradition on New Year's Eve, perhaps because it goes so nicely with champagne. Oysters on the half shell and lump crabmeat with a light rémoulade sauce (top left and top right) make elegant starters. Tiny stuffed quail (above) and a tender veal chop bathed in almond-grape sauce (opposite) are both nicely matched by seasonal side dishes, like the pureed yams in a little hollowed-out pumpkin. See pages 119–122 for the recipes.

and vegetables carefully presented makes each plate festive. Desserts drawn from family traditions can be made as sophisticated as they are heartwarming. Always choose basic ingredients you that understand, even if the twist is new. Most of all, choose foods that you love, and it's likely your guests will love them, too.

Holiday dinners at the Hope and Glory Inn in Irvington, Virginia, strike that pleasing balance, and they are always reserved months ahead of time. The owners not only transform the inn with sumptuous decorations but also translate the bounty of local foods into delectable party fare. "Whatever your region, look to the best of local ingredients," says Joyce Barber, the chef who created the dishes on these and the next two pages. Raised in the South, Joyce dips into her own family past for cherished taste-memories, then renders those old faithfuls in intriguing ways, making each plate a little artwork in itself. "Holiday time," she believes, "is all about spoiling yourself."

CHAMPAGNE CHOCOLATE TRUFFLES *An ideal confection to make as a gift or to serve with after-dinner coffee, homemade truffles (left) have a melt-in-your-mouth creaminess. These actually get their extra sparkle not from bubbly champagne but from champagne liqueur, which is sweeter. To coat them, roll the truffles in confectioners' sugar or, for variety, try cloaking some with crushed pistachios, hazelnuts, or toffee. To find the recipe and gift-packaging tips, turn to page 124.*

COMPOTE OF DRIED FRUITS
What would the holidays be without sweet dried fruits? Simmered in a port-wine syrup, this compote makes a jewel-toned topping for an old-fashioned tower of molded ice cream (opposite). It stores well, so it's easy to keep on hand. For the recipe and other serving ideas, see page 127.

TRIO OF FRESH-FRUIT COMPOTES
The bright flavors of fresh fruit are particularly welcome after a holiday meal. When poached and infused with subtle flavors, fruit gets even better. Oranges with cinnamon, pears with mint, and plums in brandy—these compotes (right) fill the bill sweetly. Turn to pages 125–127 for the three recipes.

CHARLOTTE RUSSE WITH FRESH
BERRIES *To make this perennial party
favorite, a creamy cassis-flavored custard is chilled
within a wreath of lady fingers in a springform
pan before being unmolded. A bit of gelatin
guarantees the custard's lightness and firmness;
each slice (opposite) is best served standing
upright to show off the deep filling. Add a
spoonful of fresh berries—these are white
and red raspberries—and a dollop of whipped
cream. A charlotte russe is as impressive as a
birthday cake, so it's a great finale at New Year's.
Why not present it with a sparkler (right) or a
single slim candle, then choose a lucky guest to
make a wish? For the recipe, turn to page 122.*

For the recipe, turn to page 122.

BREAD PUDDING WITH TAPIOCA
SAUCE *"My grandmother made bread
pudding with white raisins for every special
meal," recalls Joyce Barber, who slices each
serving of her own creation (left) with a star-
shaped cookie cutter. Sweet, spicy, and the
epitome of homey, this version is sauced with
another blissful treat that's sure to jog even
more childhood memories: vanilla-flavored
tapioca. For the recipe, turn to page 123.*

For the recipe, turn to page 123.

"Christmas is all about treating
the ones you love to the best there is."

—*Chef Joyce Barber*

CHAMPAGNE CHOCOLATE
TRUFFLES

An ideal confection to make as a gift or to serve with after-dinner coffee, homemade truffles (left) have a melt-in-your-mouth creaminess. These actually get their extra sparkle not from bubbly champagne but from champagne liqueur, which is sweeter. To coat them, roll the truffles in confectioners' sugar or, for variety, try cloaking some with crushed pistachios, hazelnuts, or toffee. *To find the recipe and gift-packaging tips, turn to page 124.*

COMPOTE OF DRIED FRUITS

What would the holidays be without sweet dried fruits? Simmered in a port-wine syrup, this compote makes a jewel-toned topping for an old-fashioned tower of molded ice cream (opposite). It stores well, so it's easy to keep on hand. *For the recipe and other serving ideas, see page 127.*

TRIO OF
FRESH-FRUIT
COMPOTES

The bright flavors of fresh fruit are particularly welcome after a holiday meal. When poached and infused with subtle flavors, fruit gets even better. Oranges with cinnamon, pears with mint, and plums in brandy—these compotes (right) fill the bill sweetly. *Turn to pages 125–127 for the three recipes.*

golden table settings

If you light the candles on vermeil candelabra or set out gold-handled fruit knives at dessert, you are probably admiring the sumptuous effect they lend the table. But it's nice, too, to remember how deeply gold is woven into our Christmas stories. After all, it was one of the gifts the Magi brought to the infant Jesus. And the legend of St. Nicholas begins with gold—and his compassion for a girl whose marriage prospects were bleak because she had no dowry. Through her window one night Nicholas, the fourth-century bishop of Myra, tossed a bag of gold coins, thus securing her future.

✎ This is the season to use gold-rimmed plates (opposite) that today may seem too formal for many other occasions. Mix different patterns, from the most heavily filigreed to the simplest wedding-band style. A clutch of dessert forks tied with a swirl of gold ribbon becomes a gift to untie before the conclusion of the meal.

✎ Gild the lily with ornaments given as party favors at your guests' places at the table. Look for regal shapes like crowns and cherubs (top right and right). Set them atop folded white napkins or tie each one with cord to make a splendid napkin ring. When your guests hang them on their Christmas trees in years to come, they'll recall this happy evening.

RECIPES

The recipes in this section appear in the same order in which the corresponding photographs appear in the chapters of this book. Below, for easy reference, they are listed alphabetically. The page number for the recipe is given first; the page number for the photograph is given second, in italics.

maple-glazed roasted duckling with apples

YIELD: 4 SERVINGS

One 4½- to 5-pound duckling,
  rinsed and patted dry, as much
  of the fat removed as possible

1 onion, quartered

1 celery stalk, cut into 3-inch pieces

3 garlic cloves

½ teaspoon dried savory, crumbled

½ teaspoon dried sage leaves, crumbled

Salt and freshly ground pepper to taste

⅓ cup pure maple syrup

1½ tablespoons red wine vinegar

1 tablespoon freshly squeezed lemon juice

1 tablespoon reduced-sodium soy sauce

1 tablespoon unsalted butter

2 tablespoons Dijon mustard

1 pound McIntosh apples
  (about three large apples),
  peeled, cored, and quartered

Fresh sage leaves and thyme sprigs,
  for garnish, if desired

For a menu celebrating the rich winter flavors of roasting, serve this duckling with Sweet-and-Sour Roasted Beets and Roasted Carrots with Ginger (recipes on facing page); for a fitting finale, choose one of the desserts on pages 114–18, all of which can be prepared ahead of time.

1. Preheat the oven to 450°F.

2. With the tip of a small sharp knife, gently prick the duck all over. In a bowl, stir together the onion, celery, garlic, and herbs, and season with the salt and pepper. Fill the cavity of the duck with the mixture. Set the duck, breast side up, on a rack in a roasting pan, and roast for 30 minutes. Reduce oven temperature to 300°F and roast for 1 hour, draining the fat as necessary.

3. While the duck is roasting, make the glaze: In a small saucepan set over medium-high heat, combine the maple syrup, vinegar, lemon juice, soy sauce, butter, and mustard; bring to a boil, then reduce heat and simmer for 2 minutes.

4. After the duck has roasted at 300°F for 1 hour, remove it from the oven. Surround the duck with the apples and spoon the glaze on top. Increase oven temperature to 425°F and return the duck to the oven; roast, basting frequently, for 30 minutes more, or until the duck is glazed and the apples are tender. Transfer to a warmed platter. Skim the fat from the pan juices; spoon the defatted juices over the duck and apples. Garnish with the fresh sage and thyme, if desired.

sweet-and-sour roasted beets

YIELD: 4 SERVINGS

2 pounds red beets (about 6 medium beets),
    with 1 inch of tops left on, washed

2 tablespoons olive oil

½ cup cider vinegar

⅓ cup honey

Pinch of ground cloves

2 teaspoons cornstarch

2 tablespoons Dijon mustard

Salt and freshly ground pepper to taste

1 tablespoon snipped fresh dill, plus sprigs
    for garnish, if desired

These beets are roasted, not boiled in the familiar cooking method, so they have a richer flavor, making them a nice complement to roasted meats. Leaving on a small portion of the tops enhances the presentation.

1. Preheat the oven to 400°F.

2. In a shallow baking dish, toss the beets with the oil. Roast for 1 hour, or until tender when pierced with a fork. Let cool enough to be handled, then peel and cut into half or quarter wedges.

3. In a saucepan set over medium heat, combine the vinegar, honey, cloves, and cornstarch, then bring to a boil, whisking. Reduce heat and simmer until slightly thickened. Whisk in the mustard and the salt and pepper.

4. Add the beets to the vinegar-honey sauce and stir gently to combine. Return to a simmer to heat the beets through. Transfer to a serving dish and sprinkle with snipped dill. Garnish with dill sprigs, if desired.

roasted carrots with ginger

YIELD: 4 SERVINGS

1 pound carrots, peeled and halved lengthwise

3 tablespoons unsalted butter, melted

3 teaspoons finely grated fresh ginger

Salt and freshly ground pepper to taste

1 teaspoon grated orange zest

1 cup orange juice

1 tablespoon honey

2 tablespoons minced fresh cilantro

Roasting isn't always a slow process. These flavorful carrots can be prepared, start to finish, in no more than half an hour.

1. Preheat the oven to 450°F.

2. In a shallow roasting pan, toss the carrots with 2 tablespoons of the butter, 2 teaspoons of the ginger, and the salt and pepper. Roast, turning twice, for 15 to 20 minutes, or until carrots are tender. Transfer to a warmed serving dish.

3. Add the remaining 1 tablespoon butter and 1 teaspoon ginger, the orange zest, orange juice, and honey to the roasting pan. Simmer over low heat until reduced and slightly thickened, about 5 minutes. Pour the sauce over the carrots, sprinkle with cilantro, and serve.

eggs in snow
with ginger custard sauce

YIELD: 6 SERVINGS

3 large egg whites

1 teaspoon vanilla

1/2 teaspoon ground ginger

1/2 teaspoon cream of tartar

1/8 teaspoon salt

1/2 cup superfine sugar

Ginger Custard Sauce (recipe follows)

2 tablespoons crystallized ginger,
    finely julienned, for garnish

This light dessert's name is translated from the French oeufs à la neige. *It is also known as* île flottante, *or "floating island." Prepare the Ginger Custard Sauce before making the meringues.*

1. Line a jelly-roll pan with a clean kitchen towel and set aside.

2. In the bowl of an electric mixer set on low, beat the egg whites with the vanilla, ground ginger, cream of tartar, and salt until foamy. Increase speed to high and beat in sugar, 1 tablespoon at a time, until all of the sugar has been incorporated and the mixture is stiff and glossy.

3. Fill a large sauté pan with 1 1/2 to 2 inches of water and bring to bare simmer over low heat. Using two serving spoons, mold the meringue mixture into egg shapes and poach in batches for about 2 minutes per side, or until set. With a slotted spoon, transfer to the jelly-roll pan to drain.

4. To serve, spoon Ginger Custard Sauce into each of 6 shallow soup plates and float 3 meringue eggs in each. Sprinkle with crystallized ginger.

ginger custard sauce

YIELD: 6 SERVINGS

3 ounces fresh gingerroot, sliced thin

1 cup milk

1/2 cup heavy cream

4 large egg yolks

1/4 cup sugar

1. In a saucepan set over medium heat, combine the ginger, milk, and cream; bring to a boil and remove from the heat. Set aside to infuse for at least 30 minutes.

2. Strain the gingered milk into a bowl and discard gingerroot. In another bowl, whisk together the yolks and sugar until light. While continuing to whisk, pour the gingered milk over the yolks; return mixture to saucepan. Cook over low heat, stirring until custard coats the back of a spoon.

3. Strain custard through a fine sieve into a serving bowl. Serve warm or cooled. Covered, it will keep in the refrigerator for up to 3 days.

meringue shells
with rose chantilly cream

YIELD: 6 SERVINGS

3 large egg whites

1/2 teaspoon cream of tartar

1/2 teaspoon pure vanilla extract

2/3 cup superfine sugar

1 cup heavy cream

2 tablespoons confectioners' sugar

1 to 2 teaspoons rose water, or to taste

1/2 pint raspberries

Pesticide-free rose petals, for garnish,
    if desired

Sprinkled on as a garnish, edible rose petals add a sweet, perfumey flourish to this heavenly dessert. Look for them at specialty markets. Never eat flowers that have been sprayed with pesticides, such as those from a florist.

1. Preheat the oven to 200°F. Line two baking sheets with parchment paper. Using a compass or a small bowl as a guide, draw three 3 1/2- to 4-inch circles, spaced generously apart, on each piece of parchment. Turn the parchment over so that the drawn lines do not transfer to the meringues.
2. In the bowl of an electric mixer set on low, beat the egg whites with the cream of tartar and vanilla until frothy. Increase speed to high and continue beating, adding superfine sugar 1 tablespoon at a time, until all of the sugar has been incorporated and the mixture is stiff and glossy.
3. Transfer the meringue to a large pastry bag fitted with a 1/2-inch tip. Starting at the center of each circle, pipe a tight spiral out to the perimeter, then continue piping rings over the outermost circle until the wall of the shell is three to four rings high. Repeat, forming shells on the remaining five circles.
4. Bake the meringues for 2 hours, or until crisp. They should color only very slightly. Turn oven off and leave meringues in the closed oven for an additional hour to dry. Meringues may be kept for several days in an airtight container, barring high humidity.
5. Make the Chantilly cream: In the bowl of an electric mixer, combine the cream, confectioners' sugar, and rose water, and beat until cream holds soft peaks.
6. To serve, place several raspberries in each shell and, using a spoon or a pastry bag fitted with a coupler and a star tip, fill each shell with the cream. Garnish with a sprinkle of rose petals.

almond bavarian
with poached pears

YIELD: 8 SERVINGS

1½ cups sugar, plus more for sprinkling
    into molds

2 tablespoons freshly squeezed lemon juice

3 firm-ripe pears, peeled and cored

Vegetable oil or vegetable-oil cooking spray,
    for coating molds

2 cups milk

½ cup blanched almonds, ground

2 teaspoons gelatin

3 large egg yolks

½ teaspoon almond extract

½ cup heavy cream

2 tablespoons lightly toasted sliced almonds,
    for garnish

To mold the Bavarian cream for this pretty dessert, you will need eight half-cup decorative dessert molds; as an alternative, use the same size custard cups or ramekins.

1. In a saucepan set over medium heat, combine one quart water, 1 cup sugar, and the lemon juice, and bring to a boil, stirring. Add the pears and poach them at a low simmer, turning occasionally, for 20 minutes or until just tender. Let cool in the syrup.

2. Lightly oil eight ½-cup dessert molds and sprinkle with sugar to taste. Set aside.

3. In a saucepan set over medium heat, combine the milk, almonds, and ¼ cup sugar and bring the mixture to a boil, stirring. Remove the pan from the heat and leave the mixture to infuse for 30 minutes.

4. In a heatproof bowl, sprinkle the gelatin over ¼ cup cold water; let soften for 5 minutes. Strain the almond milk through a fine sieve into another saucepan and bring just to a boil. Add the gelatin mixture and stir until dissolved. Remove from heat.

5. Have ready an ice-water bath. In the bowl of an electric mixer, beat the yolks with the remaining ¼ cup sugar on medium for 5 minutes, or until light and thick. With the mixer running, slowly pour the warm almond milk into the yolks. Place the mixing bowl in the ice-water bath to cool completely, stirring occasionally. Add the almond extract and stir to combine.

6. In a clean bowl of the electric mixer, beat the cream until it holds soft peaks. Fold the whipped cream into the almond mixture gently but thoroughly. Divide the mixture evenly among the molds and chill in the refrigerator for at least 3 hours, or until set.

7. To unmold, quickly dip each mold in warm water and invert onto a dessert plate. Slice the pears and evenly divide them among the servings; sprinkle with sliced almonds.

coconut angel food cakes

YIELD: 6 SERVINGS

1/3 cup cake flour

Pinch of salt

4 large egg whites

1/4 teaspoon cream of tartar

1/2 teaspoon almond extract

1/2 cup superfine sugar

2 tablespoons coconut milk

1 cup confectioners' sugar

1/2 cup freshly grated coconut

Fluffy drifts of freshly grated coconut atop a sweet glaze make these cakes special treats for an afternoon tea or the end of a dinner party. One medium coconut yields three to four cups grated; store extra flakes tightly covered and refrigerated for up to four days, frozen up to six months.

1. Preheat oven to 350°F. Have ready six 3/4-cup angel food cake molds.

2. Into a bowl, sift together the cake flour and salt.

3. In the bowl of an electric mixer on medium speed, beat together the egg whites, cream of tartar, and almond extract until foamy. Increase the speed to high and beat in the sugar, 1 tablespoon at a time, until the mixture is stiff and glossy.

4. Sift the flour mixture over the egg whites in two additions, folding with a rubber spatula to combine thoroughly after each addition. Spoon the batter into the molds and bake for 20 to 25 minutes. To unmold, you may need to run a knife around the edge of each cake to loosen.

5. Make the glaze: In a bowl, thoroughly combine the coconut milk with the confectioners' sugar. Drizzle the glaze over each cake and sprinkle with grated coconut.

white chocolate mousse

YIELD: 6 SERVINGS

1 teaspoon gelatin

2 tablespoons white crème de cacao

1½ cups heavy cream

6 ounces white chocolate, chopped

2- to 4-ounce block white chocolate,
    for curls to garnish

Surprisingly, white chocolate—a mixture of sugar, cocoa butter, milk solids, lecithin, and vanilla—is not officially chocolate at all because it contains no chocolate liquor. But white chocolate is an ethereal treat nonetheless and brings an unexpected quality to this mousse. For a light-and-dark contrast, make the garnish of curls from dark instead of white chocolate.

1. In a heatproof bowl, sprinkle the gelatin over the crème de cacao; let soften for 5 minutes.

2. In a small saucepan set over medium heat, bring ½ cup of the heavy cream to a simmer. Pour over the gelatin mixture and stir to dissolve. Reduce heat to low and add chopped chocolate; stir until melted and smooth. Chill, covered, for 20 minutes, or until cool and slightly thickened.

3. In the bowl of an electric mixer, beat the remaining cream to soft peaks. Whisk the cooled chocolate mixture until smooth, then gently but thoroughly fold in the whipped cream.

4. Spoon mousse into individual dessert bowls or glasses and chill for at least 2 hours, or until set.

5. Using a vegetable peeler, make curls from the block of white chocolate. Top each serving of mousse with a small shower of chocolate curls.

oysters on the half shell

YIELD: 4 SERVINGS

24 Rappahannock oysters, or other variety, as desired

Coarse crystal salt

One yellow bell pepper, seeded and diced

Use only oysters with tightly closed shells; discard any that are open. Due to potential health risks, raw seafood should not be eaten by pregnant women, babies, young children, the elderly, or anyone whose health has been compromised.

Cover each of 4 plates with enough salt to form a steadying, sandlike base for the oysters. Scrub the oyster shells. Being careful to leave all the juices in a half shell, shuck oysters; cut the meat away from the shell, but do not remove. Place 6 oysters on the half shell on top of the coarse salt on each plate; sprinkle diced yellow pepper over each. Serve immediately.

chesapeake bay blue crab cocktail with rémoulade sauce

YIELD: 4 SERVINGS

1 cup mayonnaise

¼ cup Dijon mustard

2 tablespoons chopped gherkins

1 teaspoon anchovy paste, if desired

2 tablespoons minced parsley leaves

1 pound jumbo lump crabmeat

1 teaspoon freshly squeezed lemon juice

20 leaves of Belgian endive (3 to 5 heads)

1 lemon, thinly sliced, for garnish, if desired

4 sprigs thyme, for garnish, if desired

1. Make the rémoulade sauce: In a bowl, combine the mayonnaise, mustard, gherkins, anchovy paste if desired, and parsley. Chill, covered, for several hours or overnight.

2. Carefully pick over the crabmeat to remove any remaining bits of shell. In a bowl, combine with the lemon juice and chill, covered, for 1 hour.

3. On each of four plates, arrange five endive leaves in a starburst pattern; top each starburst with a quarter of the crabmeat; spoon rémoulade sauce between the leaves. Garnish each serving with a lemon slice and a sprig of thyme, if desired.

roast stuffed quails

2/3 cup cooked blended rice

1/2 cup cooked barley

1 tablespoon melted unsalted butter

1/4 cup Madeira, or to taste

Salt and freshly ground pepper to taste

Unsalted butter, softened, to taste

6 dressed quails

Pale Madeira Sauce (recipe follows)

Sweet and delicate quails are the smallest commonly eaten game birds. You can count on one bird per guest as an appetizer or small entrée; two birds will make a more generously sized entrée.

1. Preheat the oven to 450°F. In a bowl, combine the rice, barley, melted butter, Madeira, and the salt and pepper.

2. Rinse the quails and pat them dry. Sprinkle the cavities with salt and pepper, and stuff with the rice-barley mixture. Truss the quails and rub the skin with the softened butter. Set the quails, breast side up, in a large roasting pan and roast for 5 minutes. Reduce the oven temperature to 300°F and roast for an additional 25 minutes, or until juices run clear when the leg joint is pierced. Remove the trussing strings.

3. Arrange quails on a serving platter and top with Pale Madeira Sauce.

pale madeira sauce

1/4 cup minced shallots

1 garlic clove, minced

3 tablespoons unsalted butter

1 1/2 teaspoons each fresh thyme leaves
    and minced sage leaves, or 1/2 teaspoon
    each crumbled dried thyme and sage

1 bay leaf

1/2 cup Madeira

1 cup beef stock or canned beef broth

1/2 cup heavy cream

Snipped fresh chives for garnish

Serve this sauce poured over the Roast Stuffed Quails (recipe above). It is also a perfect complement to other roasted fowl.

1. In a saucepan set over medium heat, melt 1 tablespoon butter, then add the shallots and garlic; cook until the shallots are softened. Add the herbs and Madeira and reduce the liquid for 1 minute. Add the beef stock and cream and reduce until slightly thickened.

2. Just before serving, whisk in the remaining butter, a little at a time, until incorporated. To serve, pour over the Roast Stuffed Quails and sprinkle with snipped chives.

rack of veal

YIELD: 8 SERVINGS

½ rack of veal, 5 to 6 pounds
   (about 6 chops)

1 tablespoon minced fresh thyme leaves or
   1½ teaspoons crumbled dried thyme leaves

Salt and freshly ground black pepper to taste

3 garlic cloves, minced

1 stick (½ cup) unsalted butter, melted

Almond and Green-Grape Sauce
   (recipe follows)

Ask your butcher to french the rack, a technique that leaves the short ribs attached and stripped of fat and gristle. The result will be the perfect presentation of your roast.

1. Preheat the oven to 450°F.

2. Season the veal with thyme, salt, and pepper. Cover the ends of the bones with aluminum foil to prevent charring. Transfer the meat to a roasting pan and roast for 15 minutes. Reduce oven temperature to 350°F. Sprinkle the veal with the chopped garlic and brush with the melted butter. Continue to roast for 30 to 35 minutes more, or until an instant-read thermometer registers 130°F for medium-rare meat. Let the meat rest for 10 minutes before carving. Serve with Almond and Green-Grape Sauce.

almond and green-grape sauce

YIELD: ABOUT 3½ CUPS

¼ cup unsalted butter

¼ cup slivered almonds

1 tablespoon freshly squeezed lemon juice

1 medium bunch seedless green grapes,
   separated and sliced in half

Salt to taste

Although it is suggested as an accompaniment to the Rack of Veal (recipe above), this sauce would be equally satisfying with other roasted meats, such as a crown roast or a loin roast of pork.

In a saucepan set over medium heat, melt the butter; add the almonds and cook until lightly golden. Remove from the heat and stir in the lemon juice, grapes, and salt; cook, stirring occasionally, until heated through. Serve with Rack of Veal.

pureed yams
in miniature pumpkins

YIELD: 8 SERVINGS

3¹/₂ pounds yams, peeled and
    cut into 1-inch cubes

4 tablespoons unsalted butter, softened

Salt and freshly ground pepper to taste

8 miniature pumpkins

1. Place the yams in a saucepan, cover with cold water, and add salt to taste. Bring to a boil over medium-high heat; reduce heat, cover, and simmer for 15 minutes, or until tender. Drain. In saucepan, mash the yams, beating in the butter and the salt and pepper.

2. Preheat the oven to 375°F. Cut out the tops of the pumpkins, reserving them as lids; hollow out pumpkins' centers, leaving a ¹/₂-inch-thick shell.

3. Oil a baking dish. Transfer the yams to a pastry bag fitted with a large star tip. Pipe the yams into the pumpkins. Arrange the filled pumpkins and lids on the oiled baking dish. Bake for 30 minutes, or until heated through. Serve warm, with lids leaning against the pumpkins on the plate.

charlotte russe with fresh berries

YIELD: 8 SERVINGS

One 7-ounce package ladyfingers

1 envelope unflavored gelatin

1 cup milk

¹/₃ cup sugar

4 egg yolks

2 teaspoons pure vanilla extract

2 tablespoons cassis (optional)

2 egg whites

1 cup heavy cream

Fresh berries, for garnish

Whipped cream, for garnish

1. Line the bottom and sides of a 9-inch springform pan with ladyfingers.

2. In a bowl, soften gelatin in ¹/₄ cup cold water for 5 minutes. In a saucepan, scald milk; remove from heat. Stir in gelatin mixture until dissolved.

3. In a bowl, whisk together ¹/₄ cup of the sugar and the yolks. Gradually whisk in the scalded milk and return mixture to the saucepan. Cook over medium-low heat, stirring with a wooden spoon, until custard is thick enough to coat the spoon. Remove from heat and let cool. Chill for 15 minutes, or until cold but not set. Stir in the vanilla and the cassis, if desired.

4. In the bowl of an electric mixer, beat whites with salt until they hold very soft peaks. Add remaining 2 tablespoons sugar and beat until firm.

5. In another bowl, beat cream to soft peaks. Fold whites gently but thoroughly into chilled custard. Fold the cream into the custard. Transfer the filling to the prepared springform pan and chill for 3 hours, or overnight.

6. Unmold, slice, and serve with berries and whipped cream.

bread pudding with tapioca sauce

YIELD: 8 SERVINGS

BREAD PUDDING

2^1/3 cups milk

2 tablespoons unsalted butter

2 large eggs

^{1}/3 cup sugar

^{1}/4 teaspoon salt

1 teaspoon pure vanilla extract

2 cups stale bread cubes

^{1}/2 cup raisins

^{1}/4 teaspoon ground cinnamon

TAPIOCA SAUCE

^{1}/2 cup large-pearl tapioca,
    soaked in water overnight

3^1/4 cups milk

^{1}/4 teaspoon salt

^{1}/2 cup sugar

^{1}/2 teaspoon pure vanilla extract

WHIPPED CREAM

1 cup heavy cream

2 tablespoons sugar

You can dress up this old-fashioned, moist comfort food by cutting out each portion with a star-shaped cookie cutter—or serve it the traditional way, spooned out or sliced into squares or diamonds with a knife.

1. Preheat the oven to 350°F. Butter a shallow baking dish.

2. Prepare the bread pudding: In a saucepan set over medium heat, scald the milk, then stir in the butter. In a large bowl, beat the eggs with the sugar, then whisk in the salt and the vanilla. Stir in the bread cubes, raisins, and cinnamon. Transfer the mixture to the buttered baking dish. Set the baking dish in a larger pan, add enough hot water to come halfway up the sides of the baking dish, and bake for 1 to 1^1/4 hours, or until set. Let cool to warm.

3. Make the tapioca sauce: Drain the tapioca. In a saucepan, combine with the milk, salt, and sugar and cook over moderately low heat, stirring, until the sauce is thick and the pearls are clear. Cool slightly. Stir in the vanilla extract.

4. Make the whipped cream: In a chilled bowl, combine the cream with the sugar and beat to soft peaks.

5. To serve: With a star-shaped cookie cutter, cut stars from the warm bread pudding. Transfer each star to a serving plate, top with the tapioca sauce, and garnish with the whipped cream.

champagne chocolate truffles

YIELD: 18 TRUFFLES

8 ounces semisweet chocolate,
   coarsely chopped

1/2 cup unsweetened cocoa powder

1/2 cup heavy cream

2 tablespoons unsalted butter,
   cut into small pieces

1 tablespoon champagne liqueur,
   such as Chambord

Confectioners' sugar, for coating

These sublimely textured bite-size morsels require few ingredients and are surprisingly easy to make. Experiment with different coatings, such as unsweetened cocoa powder, finely chopped nuts, or chocolate sprinkles. To give them as little gifts or favors, line shallow lidded boxes (big enough for two to six truffles each) with folded tissue or parchment and fill with truffles set in individual fluted paper candy cups. Be sure to keep them refrigerated, and remind recipients to do the same—that is, if anyone can resist eating them all at once!

1. In a food processor, combine the chocolate and cocoa; process until pulverized. Set aside.

2. In a small saucepan set over medium heat, stir together the heavy cream, butter, and liqueur until hot but not boiling. Add the mixture to the chocolate in the food processor. Process until smooth.

3. Pour the chocolate mixture into a small bowl. Cover and refrigerate for several hours, until firm enough to shape. Working with cold hands (rinse them in cold water or dip them in an ice-water bath, then dry), roll rounded teaspoons of the chocolate mixture into balls. Roll the balls in confectioners' sugar to coat and set on a baking sheet lined with waxed or parchment paper.

4. Refrigerate, covered, until 30 to 45 minutes before serving. Truffles can be stored in an airtight container in the refrigerator for up to 3 weeks.

oranges in orange syrup

YIELD: 6 SERVINGS

1½ cups sugar

6 medium seedless oranges, preferably navel

1 cinnamon stick

1 teaspoon orange flower water or
    ½ teaspoon orange extract

These cinnamon-infused whole oranges are a wonderfully refreshing dessert after a rich holiday meal. Serve them in shallow bowls or deep dessert plates and eat with a knife and fork. Cutting a thin slice off the bottom of each orange before cooking will create a flat base that keeps the orange from rolling on the plate when it is being served and eaten.

1. In a large saucepan, combine the sugar and 4 cups of water. Bring to a boil, stirring to dissolve the sugar. Boil for 10 minutes, until the syrup begins to thicken.

2. While the syrup is boiling, gently scrub the oranges under warm water. With a sharp knife or a vegetable peeler, carefully peel the thin layer of orange zest from 3 oranges. Julienne the orange zest and add to the boiling syrup.

3. Peel all 6 oranges down to the flesh, making sure you remove all of the white pith. When the syrup begins to thicken, add the oranges, cinnamon stick, and orange flower water. Reduce the heat and cover the oranges with a clean white towel to keep them submerged (add more water during cooking time, if necessary). Simmer for 10 minutes.

4. Remove the saucepan from the heat. Uncover and let the oranges and syrup cool slightly.

5. Remove the cinnamon stick. Spoon warm or cool oranges into serving dishes and pour some orange syrup over each orange; garnish with the orange zest.

Note: For easier eating, section the uncooked oranges over a bowl to catch the juice. Add the orange sections and juice to the boiled syrup as in step 3 above. Cover with a towel and simmer for 3 to 5 minutes. Continue with step 4. Eat with a spoon.

minted pears with honey walnuts

YIELD: 4 SERVINGS

2 teaspoons unsalted butter, plus more
    for cookie sheet

1/2 cup honey, plus 2 tablespoons

1/2 cup walnuts

3 bags mint tea

12 small pears, preferably Seckel or Forelle

Juice of 1 lemon

Sprigs of mint, for garnish

Christmas marks the last opportunity of the year to enjoy the petite Seckel pear, which is most readily available from late August through December. Because the pears are cooked in mint tea rather than in a liqueur, this compote is a light variation on more traditional versions.

1. Butter a small cookie sheet. In a medium-size skillet, melt the butter and 2 tablespoons of honey over medium heat. Add the walnuts. Cook, stirring often, for 5 minutes, until the nuts begin to caramelize. Spread the nut mixture on a cookie sheet to cool.

2. In a large saucepan, bring 4 cups of water to a boil; remove from heat. Add the tea bags and the remaining 1/2 cup honey, stirring to dissolve the honey. Cover and let steep for 5 minutes.

3. While the tea is steeping, peel the pears, leaving the stems intact. Rub each pear with lemon juice to prevent discoloration.

4. Remove tea bags from the tea and discard. Return the saucepan to the heat and bring tea to a simmer. Add the pears; cover and simmer for 10 to 20 minutes, until the pears are tender. (Simmering time will depend on the size and ripeness of the pears.)

5. Serve the pears, warm or cooled, in the poaching syrup. Spoon 3 pears into each of 4 serving dishes and sprinkle with the honey walnuts. Garnish with sprigs of mint.

brandied plums

YIELD: 4 SERVINGS

1 cup sugar

1 pound plums

¼ cup brandy

1 teaspoon pure vanilla extract

Granulated sugar, for garnish

So easy to prepare, this English classic is especially convenient for busy holiday hosts because it can be made ahead of time and stored, tightly covered and refrigerated, for up to a month. Try serving the plums with a little rum-raisin ice cream or a dollop of whipped cream.

1. In medium-size saucepan, bring the sugar and 2 cups water to a boil, stirring to dissolve the sugar. Boil for 10 minutes.

2. Add the plums, brandy, and vanilla. Reduce heat, cover, and simmer for 5 to 15 minutes, until tender. (Cooking time will depend on the size and ripeness of the plums.) Remove from heat, uncover, and let cool.

3. To serve, spoon the plums and syrup into serving dishes and sprinkle with granulated sugar.

compote of dried fruits with port

YIELD: 4 SERVINGS

1 cup sugar

½ cup white port wine

Juice and grated zest of 1 lemon

2 cups mixed dried fruits, such as apricots, figs, prunes, pears, and cherries

This compote is delicious served on its own in a little saucer or ladled over a scoop of vanilla ice cream. For a special treat, spoon it over freshly made waffles on Christmas morning. It can be kept, covered and refrigerated, for up to one month.

1. In a large saucepan, combine the sugar, port, lemon juice and zest, and 2½ cups water. Bring to a boil, stirring to dissolve the sugar. Add the dried fruits and reduce the heat. Cover and simmer for 10 minutes, until tender.

2. Using a slotted spoon, remove the fruit from the syrup and place it in a heatproof bowl.

3. Bring the syrup, uncovered, to a low boil. Reduce the liquid by half. Remove from heat and let cool slightly. Pour over the fruit and serve.

HANDMADE GIFTS

THERE'S NOTHING QUITE AS GRATIFYING AS CREATING YOUR OWN ORNAMENTS AND GIFTS BY

hand. Not only is there pleasure in the doing but for holiday seasons long after, your personal message of love is sure to be

recalled and cherished. Rather than scurry around for materials at the last moment, plan ahead during the year, gathering

fabric remnants, beautiful papers, ribbons and braid, buttons and shells—whatever items appeal to you and perhaps fit into

a theme you've chosen for that year's Christmas. To guarantee that your work on crafts, decorating, and wrapping will go

smoothly, make sure the tools you'll need are organized and at hand, from scissors and glue to embroidery needles and

threads. And remember, the instructions we offer here for creating a star ornament, a heart of buttons, a monogrammed

wreath, and a ribbon board for displaying cards are easily adapted to other sizes, colors, and inventive interpretations.

r i b b o n - s t a r   o r n a m e n t

To make the ribbon-star ornament shown on page 38, you will need:

3½ yards of 1½-inch-wide ribbon

Needle and thread

Two 3¼-inch disks of buckram
(or substitute stiff felt or stiff
nonwoven interfacing)

18 inches of narrow ribbon or cord

1. Cut two 24½-inch lengths and twelve 5¼-inch lengths of the 1½-inch-wide ribbon.

2. Create twelve points for the two stars (later, these two stars will be sewn back to back to form one two-sided star) by folding each 5¼-inch length of ribbon into thirds (a and b) and press. On each point, fold the left corner back (c) and secure with two stitches. This should look like the lapel of a coat. You do not need to press this part.

3. Working one at a time, attach six points to each buckram disk (d and e): Stitch them to the center of the disk to secure, also tacking the inner points of the stars to one another where they meet at the edge of the disk.

4. Leaving a ¼-inch seam allowance on the end of a 24½-inch length of ribbon, stitch the ends together to form a circle; repeat with the remaining 24½-inch length of ribbon. Mark each ribbon on both edges every 4 inches. Bringing the selvage edges together, fold the circle in half widthwise (f), stitching once where marked edges meet (for a total of six stitches). At each of these six stitches, pinch just the inner fold of ribbon together and make another stitch ½ inch away from the original stitch on only one side of the ribbon to form the six points that radiate around the circle.

5. Drawing each loop together at the center (g), stitch to secure. Holding the selvage edges against the star, attach the loop center to the star center with several stitches. Flatten the loops to form soft points (h). Use your thumb on top of the fold and your index finger below to tuck the selvages under, toward the center.

6. Knot the 18-inch length of narrow ribbon to make a loop for hanging the ornament. Stitch the knot to the buckram at one of the inner points of one of the stars, then stitch the two stars together, back to back, at their inner and outer points.

button-heart ornaments

These ornaments make appealing use of extra buttons, as well as other trinkets like charms, medals, and orphaned earrings. To turn a smaller heart into a brooch, glue a pin back (available in crafts stores) to its back. To make an ornament like those shown on page 38 and at right, you will need:

Buttons, plus other small items as desired

4-inch square of cardboard or balsa wood

5-inch square of fabric for the backing

White glue

Hot glue gun, if desired

Cord for a loop

1. Draw a heart pattern on the cardboard or balsa wood. Using a utility knife, cut out the shape.

2. Center the cardboard or balsa-wood heart on the fabric. Leaving an additional ½ inch all around the cardboard heart, draw another heart on the fabric. Using scissors, cut out the fabric heart.

3. Apply a thin, even layer of glue to one side of the cardboard. Center it, glue side down, on the fabric heart (a). Working a little bit at a time, apply glue to the outer ½ inch of the cardboard, then fold the raw edges of the fabric over and press to secure. To fold over the fabric on either side of the heart's notch, snip the fabric straight in from its notch to the notch of the cardboard heart.

4. Using small dabs of white glue or a glue gun, attach the least interesting buttons, such as flat shirt buttons, around the edge of the exposed cardboard side of the heart (b). Then build up the design from the outside to the center until the entire heart is covered.

5. Knot a loop of cord for hanging; attach it to the fabric side of the heart with glue.

a

b

friends-and-family ribbon wreath

This wreath is just as meaningful even if you monogram only some of the ribbons. Or you can enjoy the beauty of the ribbons alone, without any monograms at all. To make the wreath as shown on page 46 or similar to the antique one shown at right, you will need:

12-inch embroidery hoop

2 yards of 1-inch-wide grosgrain ribbon to wrap the hoop

Thirty-six 18-inch lengths (18 yards total) of 1- to 1½-inch-wide satin, grosgrain, or silk ribbon for the bows

Thirty-six 6½-inch lengths of ⅜-inch-wide gold ribbon (6½ yards total) for the accent knots

Embroidery floss or fine-point fabric markers

Fabric glue

1. Trace the initials 2 inches from one end of each 18-inch length of ribbon. Embroider initials in an outline stitch and make periods with a French knot (see pages 136–37), or inscribe initials with fabric markers.

2. Glue one end of the 2-yard length of grosgrain ribbon to the inside face of the embroidery hoop. Wrap the hoop with the ribbon to completely cover the wood; secure the other end of ribbon with glue.

3. Using the monogrammed ribbons, tie thirty-six bows on the wreath form, being sure to keep them evenly distributed. Tie the bows with the embroidered end of the ribbon on top of the bow and on the outside of the frame; before tightening the knots, slip a dab of glue (use a toothpick or a cotton swab) inside the knot so it will remain secure. If desired, trim the ends of the bows with a diagonal or notched cut.

4. Knot the 6½-inch lengths of ribbon between all the bows and trim the ends as desired. Hang the wreath from a hook, or attach a wire or ribbon loop for hanging.

ribbon-board screen

The folding ribbon board shown on page 49 is a 28-inch-square screen with each panel 7 inches wide. To make it, you will need:

28-inch-square piece of 3/8-inch foam core

1 yard of printed fabric for the front

1 yard of felt for the back

Approximately 8 yards of 3/4-inch-wide ribbon for latticework

Approximately 8 yards of 3/8-inch-wide ribbon or gimp for the trim

Six small reversible hinges

White glue or a hot glue gun

Spray glue

Staple gun

Small brads, if desired

1. Using a photocopier, enlarge the template on the facing page until it measures 28 inches by 7 inches (we copied it at 200%, then enlarged that copy at 175%; you'll need to tape several copies together to create the full-size template). Cut out the full-size template, then trace its shape on the foam core four times. Using a utility knife, cut the four panels from the foam core.

2. Using the template and scissors, cut four pieces of felt to the same size.

3. Add 3/4 inch to all edges of the template, then trace and cut four pieces of the printed fabric to this size.

4. Working with one panel at a time, lightly cover one side of the panel with spray glue. Carefully position the fabric and press into place. Trim off excess fabric at the corners and cut notches at the curves (a). Secure the raw edges of the fabric to the back of the panel with white glue.

5. For each panel, cut six 12-inch lengths of the 3/4-inch-wide ribbon and arrange on the fabric side of the panel in a lattice pattern, using the lines on the template as a guide. Staple the ribbon ends to the back of the panel and trim the excess ribbon as necessary.

6. Using spray glue, affix a felt piece to the back of each panel. Use white glue or a hot glue gun to cover the edges of each panel with the remaining 3/8-inch-wide ribbon or gimp.

7. Arrange the panels side by side, with the printed-fabric side down, and align their feet against a taped-down yardstick (b). Position and attach two reversible hinges between each set of panels with a hot glue gun or with small brads.

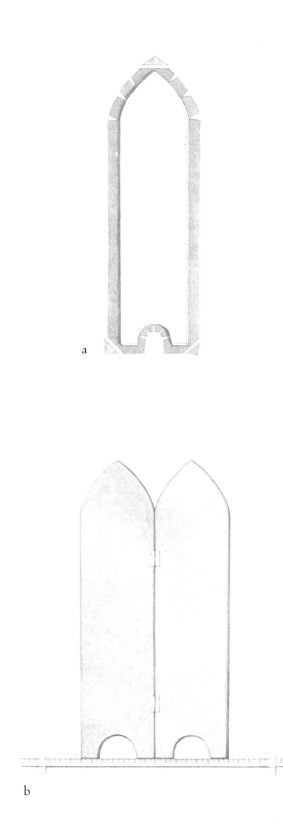

a

b

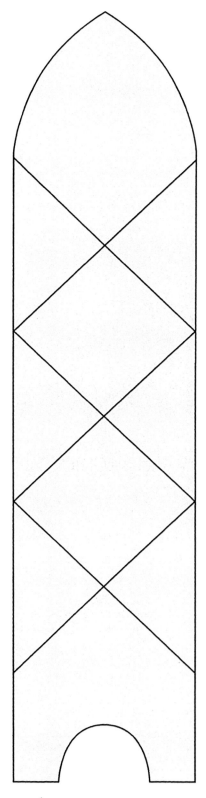

template

e m b r o i d e r y s t i t c h e s

Embroidery, the art of stitching designs on fabric, encompasses a wide range of fabrics and threads and offers a variety of finished effects. Regardless of the fabric and thread used or the gift or keepsake created, all embroidery employs the same stitches. Included on these pages is a sampling of the most popular of those stitches. The outline stitch, chain stitch, and French knot can all be used to monogram the ribbons for the wreath on pages 46 and 133. The others can be used to adorn a variety of gifts, as suggested on page 47.

OUTLINE OR STEM STITCH

STRAIGHT STITCH

CHAIN STITCH

SATIN STITCH

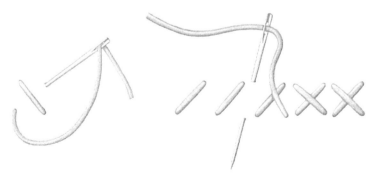

CROSS-STITCH

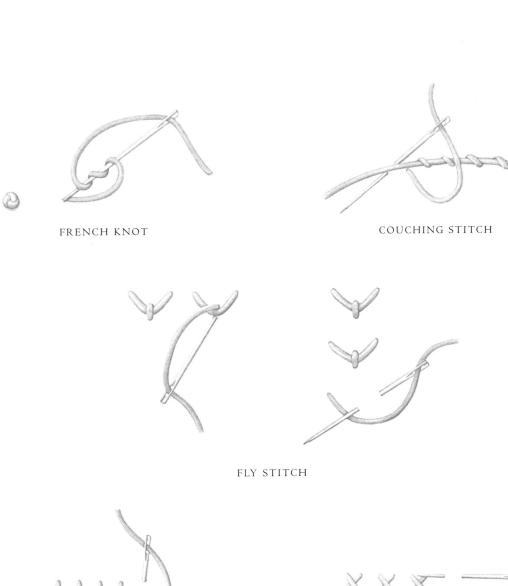

FRENCH KNOT

COUCHING STITCH

FLY STITCH

BUTTONHOLE STITCH

HERRINGBONE STITCH

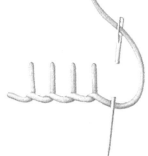

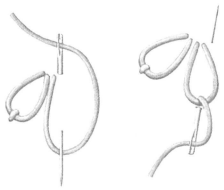

LAZY DAISY STITCH

FEATHER STITCH

RESOURCES

The following is a chapter-by-chapter listing of sources for many of the items pictured in this book. Every effort has been made to ensure the accuracy of addresses, telephone numbers, and Internet addresses, but these may change after going to press.

WHITE WINTER'S EVE

page 16
Wallpaper-covered bandboxes from Hannah's Treasures, 1101 Seventh Street, Harlan, IA 51537; (712) 755-3173 or www.hannahstreasures.com.

Ruffled seat cover from Paper White, (415) 457-7673 or www.pwlinens@aol.com.

page 17
Porcelain-and-organza angel from the Jim Marvin Collection, (615) 441-1015 for nearest retailer.

page 18 (top)
Dessert stand, crystal-and-silver biscuit jar, and *tray* from Michael Feinberg Inc., (212) 532-0311.

White-frosted petit fours from Kathleen's Bake Shop, 43 North Sea Road, Southampton, NY 11968; (631) 283-7153 or www.kbsonline.com.

page 18 (bottom)
Stockings sewn by Sandra Dunn, Sandra Dunn Fine Linens and Laces, 58 Stephen Street, Manchester, CT 06040; (860) 647-1812.

Vintage buttons from Tender Buttons, 143 East 62nd Street, New York, NY 10021; (212) 758-7004.

page 19
Ivory silk roses from Dulken & Derrick Inc., 12 West 21st Street, New York, NY 10010; (212) 929-3614 or www.topsilks.com.

Ribbons from Vaban Gille, (415) 552-5490 for nearest retailer.

Ornaments from Merck Family's Old World Christmas, (800) 965-7669 or www.oldworldchristmas.com for nearest retailer.

page 20 (left)
Jars and *candy* from Be-Speckled Trout, 422 Hudson Street, New York, NY 10014; (212) 255-1421.

page 21
Ornaments on top and bottom shelf from Merck Family's Old World Christmas, see above.

Ornaments on bottom shelf from Peter Priess, Kegelgasse 27, A-1030 Wien, Austria; 011-43-1-714-92-20 or fax 011-43-1-712-43-95 for U.S. retailers.

page 22
"Sheer Rapture" wired ribbon from Vaban Gille, see above.

page 25
Wallpaper-covered bandbox from Hannah's Treasures, see above.

page 26
Antique linens from Antique European Linens, 14 North Palafox Street, Pensacola, FL 32501; (800) 444-0594, www.antiqueeuropeanlinens.com, www.decadencedown.com, or ael@dotstar.net.

Colin Cowie Collection goblets (with lemon slices) from Lenox, (800) 635-3669 or www.lenox.com for nearest retailer.

"Malmaison" silver flatware from Christofle, (800) 799-6886 for nearest retailer.

page 27 (top and middle)
"White Full Lace" china serving dishes from Royal Copenhagen, (800) 431-1992 for nearest retailer.

page 28 (right)
"Cameo White" soup bowl and *dinner plate* from Villeroy & Boch, (800) 845-5376.

page 29
"Georgia" serving plate by Jean Louis Coquet available through Lalique, (800) 993-2580 or www.lalique.com for nearest retailer.

"Octavie" crystal flute from Villeroy & Boch, see above.

page 30
"White Full Lace" china from Royal Copenhagen, see above.

Colin Cowie Collection goblets from Lenox, see above.

HEIRLOOM CHRISTMAS

page 38
Ribbons available from Bell'occhio, 8 Brady Street, San Francisco, CA 94103; (415) 864-4048.

pages 40–45
Glass balls from Maville at Bon Marché, 22 Rue De Sèvres, 75005 Paris; 011-33-1-44-39-80-00.

page 40
Chandelier from Blanc d'Ivoire, 104 Rue Du Bac, 75007 Paris; 011-33-1-45-44-41-17.

page 41
Votive holders, candlestick with crystal drops, and *antique silver balls* from Le Monde Sauvage, 101 Rue St. Denis, 75001 Paris; 011-33-1-40-26-28-92.

page 43
Fabric from Diaspree, 27 Rue De Bourgogne, 75005 Paris; 011-33-1-45-51-39-06.

page 44

Glasses from Le Cèdre Rouge,
116 Rue Du Bac, 75007 Paris;
011-33-1-42-84-84-00.

Porcelain plates from Yves Hallard,
252 Bis Boulevard St. Germain,
75007 Paris; 011-33-1-42-22-60-50.

Tablecloth from Diaspree, see above.

Vermeil flatware and *salver* from
Odiot, 7 Place de la Madeleine,
75008 Paris; 011-33-1-42-65-00-95.

page 45

Vermeil flatware from Odiot,
see above.

Red silk quilted blanket (used as
tablecloth), *candlesticks,* and *glass
servers* from Blanc d'Ivoire, see above.

page 47

*Star coated in antique German
glitter* from Theatre of Dreams,
P.O. Box 20, Port Costa, CA 94569;
(510) 787-2164.

Candle by At-Choo, (310) 278-5987
or (877) 234-6941.

A G A R D E N E R ' S
H O L I D A Y

page 52

Wreaths from White Flower Farm,
P.O. Box 50, Litchfield,
CT 06759; (800) 503-9624
or www.whiteflowerfarm.com.

page 53

Four-tiered flower vase from
The Tulip Tree Collection,
34 Route 47, Washington Depot,
CT 06794; (860) 868-2802.

Cream-glazed pot from Potluck
Studios, (914) 626-2300 for
nearest retailer.

Planter stand by Lexington Furniture
Industries, The Smithsonian
Anniversary Collection, available from
The Tulip Tree Collection, see above.

page 55

Wreaths from White Flower Farm,
see above.

Tree and *other evergreens*
from Green Valley Growers,
P.O. Box 1372, Sebastopol, CA
95473; (707) 823-5583.

Topiaries from Litchfield Hills
Nursery, 393 Torrington Road,
Route 202, Litchfield, CT 06759;
(860) 567-9374.

*Settee, baker's rack, wicker
hamper,* and *needlepoint pillows*
from The Tulip Tree Collection,
see above.

Wire cage (on baker's rack) from
Vance Kitira International, (800)
646-6360 for nearest retailer.

Green throw from Hayseed,
P.O. Box 566, Litchfield, CT 06759;
(860) 567-8775.

Wardian case from Debra Queen,
354 Elms Street, South Dartmouth,
MA 02748; (508) 991-3106.
By appointment.

page 56

Wire basket from The Big
Greenhouse, 3600 Spring Garden
Street, Greensboro, NC 27407;
(336) 852-4451.

page 57

Ladder-back chairs and
antique table from The Tulip
Tree Collection, see above.

Plates and *flatware* from Vance
Kitira International, see above.

Seed ornaments from Loose Ends, 3824 River Road North, Keizer, OR 97303; (503) 390-7457 or www.looseends.com for catalog or nearest retailer.

page 59

Amaryllises from White Flower Farm, see above.

page 60 (right)

Lidded glass jars from Williams-Sonoma, (800) 541-2233 or www.williams/sonoma.com.

T E A   P A R T Y
I N   P A S T E L S

page 64

Brocade-upholstered chairs from Julia Gray Ltd., 979 Third Avenue, New York, NY 10022; (212) 223-4454. To the trade.

pages 64–68

Sugar-paste ornaments by Betty Van Norstrand, 6 Leonard Road, Poughkeepsie, NY 12601; (914) 471-3386 for information about sugar-paste decorations and sugar-work classes.

Blown-glass ornaments and blown-glass garlands from D. Blümchen & Company, P.O. Box 1210-V, Ridgewood, NJ 07451; (201) 652-5595 or www.blumchen.com.

Glass-rose ornaments from Merck Family's Old World Christmas, (800) 965-7669 or www.oldworldchristmas.com for nearest retailer.

page 67

Wallpaper-covered bandboxes from Hannah's Treasures, 1101 Seventh Street, Harlan, IA 51537; (712) 755-3173 or www.hannahstreasures.com.

page 69 (top)

Antique china from Chrystian Aubusson Inc., 315 East 62nd Street, New York, NY 10021; (212) 755-2432.

Silver tray from Michael Feinberg Inc., (212) 532-0311.

page 71

Three-tiered dessert stand from English Country Antiques, Snake Hollow Road, Bridgehampton, NY 11932; (631) 537-0606 or ecantiques@aol.com.

W H I M S Y   I N
T H E   S N O W

pages 74–86

Paper tree topper from The Moravian Bookshop, 428 Main Street, Bethlehem, PA 18018; (610) 866-5481 or www.moravianstar.com.

Red-ball, icicle, and birdhouse ornaments from Midwest of Cannon Falls, 32057 64th Avenue, P.O. Box 20, Cannon Falls, MN 55009; (800) 776-2075.

Striped heart ornaments from Vietri, (919) 732-5933 or www.vietri.com for preferred retailers.

Starfish ornaments from John Derian, 6 East 2nd Street, New York, NY 10003; (212) 677-3917.

page 76

Porcelain fruit from Department 56, (800) 548-8696 or www.department56.com for nearest retailer.

pages 77, 78

Reticulated urn from Royal Creamware USA, 76 Broad Street, Guilford, CT 06437; (800) 717-4135.

page 77

Flatware from Lunt Silversmiths, (413) 774-2774 for nearest retailer.

Crystal goblets from Villeroy & Boch, (800) 845-5376.

Hurricane lamps from Zodax, (818) 785-5626 for nearest retailer.

Fringed chenille blanket (used as tablecloth) from Textillery, (812) 334-1555 or www.textillery.com for nearest retailer.

Swans Island Blanket handwoven by Atlantic Blanket Company, (207) 526-4492, (888) 526-9526, or www.atlanticblanket.com.

page 79 (top left)

Shortbread heart cookies from Christopher's Desserts at Brandow's and Co., 340 Warren Street, Hudson, NY 12534; (518) 822-8938.

page 81 (bottom)

Plates from Royal Creamware USA, see above.

page 83

Taffeta stocking from Bravura at the Loom Company, (212) 366-7214 for nearest retailer.

'TIS THE SILVER SEASON

pages 88, 89

Cookie ornaments by Patti Paige of Baked Ideas, 450 Broadway, New York, NY 10013; (212) 925-9097.

pages 90 (bottom), 91

Lace cloth and *napkins* from Sandra Dunn Fine Linens and Laces, Manchester, CT; (860) 646-4002. By appointment.

page 92

Stocking from Sandra Dunn Fine Linens and Laces, see above.

Bird-shaped candle from Illuminée du Monde, 394 Rockydale Road, Bristol, VT 05443; (800) 322-2660.

page 95

Plaid silk taffeta from Schumacher, (800) 332-3384.

Antique lace tablecloth from Second Chance, Southampton, NY; (516) 283-2988.

page 97

Vintage cards from Second Chance, see above.

A GLORIOUS GLOWING FEAST

page 100

Christmas tree decorated by John Taylor, Silk Jungle, 3429 West Cary Street, Richmond, VA 23221; (804) 359-5993.

"Darjeeling" champagne-colored tablecloths from Palais Royale, (800) 322-3911.

page 105 (right)

Linen-and-cotton napkins embroidered with wheat sheaves, tasseled runner, silver-plated champagne bucket, and *footed crystal fruit bowl* from Salamagundi Antiques, Gifts & Stationery at Kilmarnock Antique Gallery, Kilmarnock, VA 22482; (800) 497-0083 or www.virginia-antiques.com.

page 106 (bottom), 107

Antique compotes from Bardith, Ltd., 901 Madison Avenue, New York, NY 10021; (212) 737-3775.

picture credits